SAC
IN THE 1980s

Adrian Symonds

AMBERLEY

Acknowledgements

I would like to thank Sally Tunnicliffe for her assistance. Special thanks go to my wife, Louise, and son, Charlie.

This book is dedicated to the men and women who served in Strategic Air Command.

First published 2022

Amberley Publishing
The Hill, Stroud
Gloucestershire, GL5 4EP

www.amberley-books.com

Copyright © Adrian Symonds, 2022

The right of Adrian Symonds to be identified as the Author of this work has been asserted in accordance with the Copyrights, Designs and Patents Act 1988.

ISBN 978 1 4456 9870 0 (print)
ISBN 978 1 4456 9871 7 (ebook)

British Library Cataloguing in Publication Data.
A catalogue record for this book is available from the British Library.

Typesetting by SJmagic DESIGN SERVICES, India.
Printed in the UK.

Contents

SAC Bases Map   4

The History and Role of SAC   5

SAC Structure   24

End of an Era   84

Bibliography   85

Appendix I: SAC Structure January 1980   87

Appendix II: SAC Structure January 1989   92

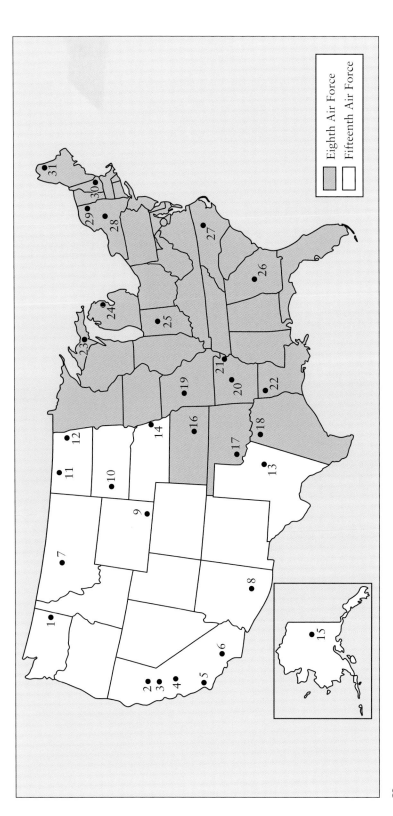

Key

1) Fairchild AFB
2) Beale AFB
3) Mather AFB
4) Castle AFB
5) Vandenberg AFB
6) March AFB, 15th AF HQ
7) Malmstrom AFB
8) Davis-Monthan AFB

9) Francis E. Warren AFB
10) Ellsworth AFB
11) Minot AFB
12) Grand Forks AFB
13) Dyess AFB
14) Offutt AFB, SAC HQ
15) Eielson AFB
16) McConnell AFB

17) Altus AFB
18) Carswell AFB
19) Whiteman AFB
20) Little Rock AFB
21) Blytheville/Eaker AFB
22) Barksdale AFB, 8th AF HQ
23) K. I. Sawyer AFB
24) Wurtsmith AFB

25) Grissom AFB
26) Robins AFB
27) Seymour Johnson AFB
28) Griffiss AFB
29) Plattsburgh AFB
30) Pease AFB
31) Loring AFB

Eighth Air Force
Fifteenth Air Force

The History and Role of SAC

Strategic Air Command (SAC), headquartered at Offutt Air Force Base (AFB), Nebraska, was a United States Air Force (USAF) Major Command (MAJCOM). Reflecting SAC's critical responsibilities, it was also a United States Department of Defense (DoD) Specified Command, meaning it was directly 'commanded' by the Secretary of Defense (SecDef), through the Joint Chiefs of Staff (JCS). Therefore, the chain of command from President of the United States (POTUS) as commander-in-chief to the Commander in Chief SAC (CINCSAC) bypassed the usual steps of the Secretary of the Air Force, and the Chief of Staff, USAF, that would otherwise be the case for most MAJCOMs.

Established under the Army Air Forces on 21 March 1946, SAC predated the USAF (established 18 September 1947) by eighteen months. SAC was responsible for America's land-based strategic bomber and intercontinental ballistic missile (ICBM) strategic nuclear arsenal, also controlling supporting infrastructure, including tanker, strategic reconnaissance and airborne command post (ABNCP) aircraft. SAC was responsible for two of the strategic 'nuclear triad' components, the third leg being the US Navy (USN) submarine-launched ballistic missiles (SLBMs).

SAC's deterrent role was reflected in its famous motto, 'Peace is Our Profession'. SAC was highly autonomous and self-sufficient, jealously guarding its assets and resisting their diversion to duties unrelated to its core mission. Although SAC could have been committed to conventional or nuclear operations against any of America's enemies (and was committed to conventional operations in Korea and Vietnam), its primary focus was strategic nuclear warfare against the Soviet Union.

SAC was administratively organised into several Numbered Air Forces, at its height controlling four. Sixteenth Air Force was the shortest lived, assigned 1957–66, controlling SAC forces in Morocco and Spain. The post-Vietnam drawdown saw Second Air Force inactivate on 1 January 1975, subsequently leaving Eighth Air Force (8th AF) and Fifteenth Air Force (15th AF), respectively, controlling SAC units in the eastern and western halves of the United States.

The Carter administration cancelled the B-1 bomber programme in 1977, deciding instead to develop air-launched cruise missiles (ALCM), allowing the B-52 to launch from 'stand-off' positions outside Soviet air defences. Development of new ICBM/SLBMs and the secret Advanced Technology Bomber (ATB) was also launched.

By 1980 B-52D/G/H heavy bombers served alongside FB-111A medium bombers. The B-52Ds retired in 1983; B-52Gs would begin a slow withdrawal at the decade's end. The AGM-86B ALCM went on alert from 1982. President Reagan resurrected the B-1 programme in 1981, due to concerns about ATB development delays; B-1Bs entered service during 1986. The ATB resulted in the revolutionary stealthy B-2A. First flying in 1989, it did not enter service until 1993 – after the Cold War's conclusion and SAC's inactivation.

In 1981, President Reagan resurrected the B-1, 240 of which had been cancelled by President Carter in 1977, through the Long Range Combat Aircraft (LRCA) programme. The 100 new B-1Bs would be considerably different to the original B-1s (retrospectively redesignated B-1As). The B-1B's Radar Cross Section (RCS) was reduced by 85 per cent through engine inlet redesign. B-1A had been optimised for high-altitude, high-speed flight; the B-1B's mission would be low-altitude penetration. This is 74-0159, the second of four B-1A prototypes, here modified to support the B-1B programme. While retaining the B-1A airframe structure, including the crew escape capsule, rather than ejection seats (the latter only introduced in the fourth B-1A), it was otherwise equipped to B-1B standard, as was the fourth prototype, 76-0174. Seen taxiing at Edwards AFB, CA, it first flew there after modification to approximate B-1B standard on 23 March 1983. (National Archives and Records Administration)

A 43d SW B-52D heading into the sunset, literally as well as figuratively, shortly before the B-52D's retirement. B-52Ds were considerably modified for use in the conflict in South East Asia. Conventional bomb capacity was drastically increased through rearrangement of the bomb bay and rewiring of underwing pylons for bomb carriage. Much improved electronic countermeasures equipment was also introduced. These improvements saw them linger in service after the war's end until 1983, outliving later models, such as the B-52F, which retired in 1978. The B-52D's withdrawal left the B-52G and B-52H models in service. (NARA)

A B-1B during a 1987 acceptance flight, conducted by Detachment 15 of the Air Force Contract Management Division, under Air Force Systems Command, prior to handover to SAC. The B-1B was externally differentiated from the B-1A by its ogival nose and rounded tail cone, which replaced the B-1A's pointed nose and tail cone; simplified intakes replaced the B-1A's moveable air ramps. While reducing the RCS, the redesigned intakes also reduced speed from Mach 2.22 (1390 mph/2236.9 km/h) for the B-1A to Mach 1.25 (792 mph/1274.6 km/h) for the B-1B at 50,000 feet. However, the B-1B's low-level penetration role made the speed decrease irrelevant. (NARA)

The first development B-2A Advanced Technology Bomber, 82-1066, during formal roll-out on 22 November 1988 at Air Force Plant 42, Palmdale, California. Initiated by President Carter in 1979, the B-2 was the pinnacle of SAC's 1980s 'Strategic Modernization Program', with 132 planned to join SAC. Its very low RCS was intended to allow it to penetrate Soviet air defences unobserved. Its intended primary mission was the destruction of high value strategic targets such as nuclear warfighting command posts, launch control centres and ICBM silos; secondary roles were hunting down mobile ICBMs, strategic defence suppression, conventional strike and maritime operations. By the time it entered service the Cold War was over and SAC had inactivated; only twenty-one were produced, including refurbished development airframes. (NARA)

A competitive fly-off was conducted from July 1979 until February 1980 between the General Dynamics AGM-109 (derived from the USN's BGM-109 Tomahawk surface-/submarine-launched cruise missile) and the Boeing AGM-86B (an enlarged and improved development of its initial AGM-86A design) to select an Air Launched Cruise Missile for SAC. Seen here in 1979, a B-52G carries a load of AGM-109s, one of which it has just released over the Utah Test and Training Range (UTTR). Ten of each missile were test fired; four of each were failures. (NARA)

An AGM-86B ALCM over the UTTR in 1980 during the fly-off. Early tests saw AGM-86Bs and AGM-109s fly repeated orbits around a 100-mile by 30-mile course over the UTTR. Later tests were launched over the Pacific, flying over California and Nevada back to Utah, followed by F-4E chase planes that could take control of the missiles in an emergency. The AGM-109B won – it was considered a superior, better engineered, design. It could also fly closer to rough terrain without losing targeting accuracy. The operational AGM-86B's W80 warhead was variable between 5 and 170 kt. (NARA)

A B-52G launches an AGM-86B over the UTTR during 1982 AGM-86 Integrated Weapon System tests. After cancelling the B-1, the Carter administration had considered using modified airliners, such as Boeing 747s and McDonnell Douglas DC-10s, as ALCM carriers, as well as B-52s. The modified airliner plans came to nothing. Eventually ninety-eight B-52Gs (of 167 remaining) and all ninety-six surviving B-52Hs were equipped to handle AGM-86Bs. When the B-1B entered service it was intended to be used as a penetration bomber, and lacked ALCM capability. However, from 1987 B-1Bs also began being tested with ALCMs. (NARA)

SAC's bomber mission was impossible without supporting tankers. Jet-powered KC-135As entered service in 1957, becoming SAC's primary tanker for the remainder of the Cold War. During the 1980s two upgrade programmes got underway, primarily replacing the J57 turbojets with more efficient turbofans. SAC KC-135As became KC-135Rs, gaining modern CFM56 (F108) turbofans. Meanwhile, Air National Guard (ANG) and Air Force Reserve (AFRES) KC-135As (which were SAC-gained in wartime) became KC-135Es, receiving JT3D (TF33) turbofans reclaimed from retired Boeing 707 airliners. In 1977 the DC-10 was selected as the basis for a new tanker/transport under the Advanced Tanker Cargo Aircraft Program, which entered service in 1981 as the KC-10A. KC-10As featured much increased fuel-offload capacity compared to KC-135s, while being air-refuellable (a capability most KC-135s lacked). SAC KC-10As often supported fighter deployments overseas, their range/fuel offload and considerable transport capacity (allowing them to carry the deployment's support equipment) making them appropriate for this role.

The large liquid-fuelled LGM-25C Titan II ICBM entered service in 1963. While earlier ICBMs had to be fuelled before launch, Titan II's storable propellant allowed launch within 60 seconds. Titan II was retained right through to 1987 due to carrying the largest US ICBM warhead, the 9 megaton W-53. The solid-fuelled Minuteman I entered service in 1962 and retired by 1974. This left LGM-30F Minuteman II and LGM-30G Minuteman III (which entered service respectively in 1965 and 1970) as the primary ICBMs. Minuteman II was armed with a 1.2-W56 warhead, and Minuteman III with either three 170-kiloton W62 or three 335–350-kiloton W78 warheads. Minuteman introduced the ability to be launched from their silos via radio signals from EC-135 ABNCP aircraft in an emergency. In 1981 President Reagan endorsed continuing development of the M-X ICBM, which emerged as the LGM-118A Peacekeeper, featuring ten 300-kiloton W87 warheads.

A new underground command post was constructed at Offutt AFB, replacing the crowded and obsolete original one, in use since 1957. The new SAC Command Center became operational in March 1989. The two-level structure, with 14,000 square feet of floor space, housed the information management and communication systems that allowed CINCSAC to command and control his forces worldwide. Its state-of-the-art computers and communications equipment were protected against damage by electromagnetic pulse (EMP) from high altitude nuclear bursts. It was also connected

The KC-10A Extender was selected to satisfy the USAF's Advanced Tanker Cargo Aircraft Program requirement. Derived from the DC-10-30CF, sixty were ordered. Having first flown on 12 July 1980, the first KC-10A is seen during initial air refuelling trials in October 1980, still carrying its civil registration N110KC, rather than its assigned USAF serial 90433 (79-0433). It is refuelling C-5A 80216 (68-0216) of MAC's 60th Military Airlift Wing. The KC-10A formally entered USAF service in March 1981. (NARA)

An LGM-118A Peacekeeper test launch from a Vandenberg AFB silo during 1989. After the initial fifty Peacekeepers equipped 400th SMS, 90th SMW, at Francis E. Warren AFB, plans existed for a further fifty to equip the same wing's 319th SMS. However, Congress intervened in July 1985, limiting Peacekeeper numbers to fifty, until more survivable basing plans could be developed. On 19 December 1986 the Reagan administration announced the basing solution for the additional fifty missiles: the Peacekeeper Rail Garrison. This was intended to use twenty-five trains, each with two Peacekeepers, stationed at various USAF facilities, but deploying onto the national railroad network to improve survivability during periods of international tension. In 1989 it was decided to limit Peacekeeper procurement to the first fifty missiles, but to redeploy them from silos to the rail garrison. The Cold War ended before these plans could be enacted and they remained in their silos. (NARA)

to ICBM and SLBM attack warning systems. Computer consoles at each staff position and eight computer-driven wall screens immediately informed the battle staff of any force status changes.

SAC had the most personnel of any USAF MAJCOM. By 1980 SAC had 118,193 personnel (18,575 officers, 85,401 airmen and 14,217 civilians). This total peaked at 122,697 by 1982, fell to 118,484 by 1984, rose again to 121,730 by 1986, declining to 117,879 by 1988 and 112,780 by 1989.

SAC held 406 bombers (343 B-52D/G/Hs and sixty-three FB-111As) in 1980, dropping to 286 (233 B-52G/Hs, fifty-one FB-111As and two B-1Bs) by 1986 and peaking at 411 (258 B-52G/Hs, fifty-nine FB-111As and ninety-four B-1Bs) in 1988. In 1980 SAC held 517 (KC-135) tankers, peaking at 556 (506 KC-135s and fifty KC-10As) in 1986, with 545 (487 KC-135s and fifty-eight KC-10As) by 1989. Between 1980 and 1985 there were a further 128 ANG/AFRES (SAC-gained) KC-135s, rising to 134 by 1989. In 1980 SAC held thirty-eight strategic reconnaissance aircraft, rising to fifty-five by 1985 and sixty-eight by 1989. For most of the decade SAC held thirty-one ABNCPs. In 1980 SAC held 1,223 ICBMs (fifty-six Titan II and 1,167 Minuteman), declining to 1,149 (nine Titan II and 1,140 Minuteman) by 1986, rising to 1,202 (1,152 Minuteman, fifty Peacekeeper) by 1989. Finally, in 1980 SAC held 1,383 air-launched missiles (all AGM-69 SRAM short-range attack missiles), rising with service-entry of ALCMs, having 2,518 (1,309 SRAM and 1,209 ALCM) by 1984 and peaking at 2,638 (1,138 SRAM and 1,500 ALCM) in 1988, before declining.

Nuclear weapons handling, including weapons release, was governed by the 'two-man rule', designed to prevent accidental or malicious launch of nuclear weapons by a single individual. All personnel handling nuclear weapons were continuously evaluated for adherence to Personnel Reliability Program (PRP) standards, ensuring they demonstrated the required high degree of individual reliability.

Nuclear War

The Joint Strategic Target Planning Staff (JSTPS), co-located with SAC headquarters and including representatives of all branches of the armed forces, planned and maintained the classified, annually reviewed, Single Integrated Operational Plan (SIOP). SIOP integrated the capabilities of SAC's bombers and ICBMs, and USN SLBMs, giving the president targeting options, describing launch procedures and targets. SIOP defined targets, allocated weapons to targets and stipulated timing. It covered mutual support and defence suppression, for example nuclear weapons destroying enemy air defences, allowing other nuclear weapons to be delivered to deeper targets. It considered deconfliction, avoiding fratricide, ensuring one nuclear weapon striking its target did not interfere with, or destroy, another nuclear weapon heading to another target. It detailed routes bombers would take to targets, for survivability against enemy defences and deconfliction. Various versions of the plan allowed the president to order different levels of attack, and options to include or exclude various countries or regions in any attack.

The National Strategic Target List (NSTL) included Soviet ICBM fields (and their command and control facilities), bomber (and other) airfields, ballistic-missile submarine bases, air defences, supply depots, military storage facilities, political centres, command posts, communications facilities, military equipment factories, refineries, steel and aluminium plants, and power plants. The Reagan administration increased SIOP's counterforce focus, prioritising the targeting of Soviet strategic nuclear forces, aided by development of more accurate and survivable systems. Part of the rationale behind the in-development ATB/B-2 was to counter mobile Soviet ICBMs, which required manned bombers to locate and destroy them.

The triad elements complimented each other. ICBMs were fast (30 minutes' flight time) and accurate, primarily used for counterforce; bombers (launched upon warning of attack) and USN SLBMs (in hard-to-detect ballistic missile submarines-SSBNs) both provided survivable second-strike capabilities in the face of an enemy first strike. Bombers, unlike ICBMs or SLBMs, offered added flexibility as they could be recalled. In the event of a Soviet nuclear attack against the United States, SAC's surviving ICBMs could target Soviet ICBM silos, both those unused in the first strike and those used and awaiting reloading for reuse. SAC bombers could make precision nuclear strikes on targets that escaped the ICBMs' warheads. USN SLBMs could be held in reserve as a secure second-strike force, primarily targeted against population centres.

In peacetime all operational SAC bomber/tanker squadrons maintained half of their aircraft on 15-minute ground alert, fuelled and nuclear-armed, with crews on standby, reducing vulnerability to a Soviet missile strike. They could be 'minimum interval take-off' (MITO) launched, with bombers/tankers at each location launching at 12–30 second intervals, allowing SAC to become airborne within minutes. In periods of international tension additional aircraft could be brought to alert. CINCSAC could order the launch of SAC's ground-alert aircraft, but only the president (or his successor) could authorise nuclear weapons release. After MITO launch, aircraft could be flown to alternate dispersal airfields (for added survivability) to sit alert, or held in airborne alert. CINCSAC could order the aircraft to proceed on their SIOP routes under 'positive control', not passing their 'fail-safe' points. Upon express orders from the president (or successor), CINCSAC could have ordered his ICBMs to be launched and bombers to proceed beyond their fail-safe points to their targets. If such an order was given, ICBMs would hit Soviet targets first; bombers would proceed at high altitude over the Arctic Circle, refuelling from tankers, before dropping to low level to penetrate Soviet air defences and hitting their targets. The bombers would take advantage of the disruption caused to Soviet air defences in the initial ICBM strike. After egressing Soviet airspace, surviving bombers would either recover to the US or divert to air bases in Europe or elsewhere, reconstituting ahead of possible further strikes. With the adoption of ALCMs in the 1980s, B-52s increasingly found themselves able to deliver warheads to targets without needing to penetrate Soviet airspace; B-1Bs took on the penetration role alongside FB-111As.

SAC's Post Attack Command and Control System (PACCS) included EC-135 ABNCPs, which co-ordinated the nuclear response and could launch ICBMs via radio signals if their ground Launch Control Centers were destroyed or incapacitated.

Strategic Reconnaissance

In peacetime SAC's strategic reconnaissance aircraft performed Peacetime Airborne Reconnaissance Program (PARPRO) overt peripheral missions in international airspace around potentially hostile nations' borders, with a particular focus on the Soviet Union and Warsaw Pact (WarPac) nations. SAC's primary reconnaissance interest was in relation to SIOP, gathering intelligence on Soviet defences, possible targets and ingress/egress routes. In wartime, they could provide pre-strike reconnaissance and post-strike Bomb Damage Assessment (BDA). Naturally, SAC found itself being regularly tasked to conduct strategic reconnaissance for other USAF MAJCOMs, other US services and agencies outside DoD.

Conventional Operations

Concern that Soviet/WarPac forces could overrun North Atlantic Treaty Organization (NATO) forces in Europe, while the US may withhold tactical nuclear weapons release, prompted SAC to develop conventional bombing operational plans to support NATO from 1976. Conventional bombing by B-52Ds, and from 1982 B-52Gs, was intended to contain Soviet/WarPac forces during any invasion of Western Europe. SR-71s and U-2s would have provided pre-strike targeting and post-strike BDA. This NATO-support tasking was known as 'Busy Brewer'; several Busy Brewer exercises occurred each year, with deployments to RAF Upper Heyford, RAF Marham, RAF Brize Norton and RAF Fairford (exclusively to the latter from late 1984). There were also non-stop Busy Brewer training flights from the US. From 1988, Busy Brewer only referred to the NATO-support mission tasking; the deployments themselves became Busy Warrior and the exercises became Mighty Warrior.

The Rapid Deployment Joint Task Force (RDJTF) activated on 1 March 1980 at MacDill AFB, Florida, following the 1979 Soviet invasion of Afghanistan, focused on deploying US forces from all services to the Middle East in a crisis, primarily the Persian Gulf region. Bright Star exercises (primarily in Egypt) practised deploying earmarked forces to the region. SAC's RDJTF contribution was the Strategic Projection Force (SPF), formed from 57th AD (5th and 319th BMW) B-52Hs/KC-135s; SR-71s, U-2Rs

A 22d BMW B-52D, deployed from March AFB, California, approaches RAF Brize Norton, UK, on 25 August 1980 during exercise Busy Brewer. (Mike Freer – Touchdown Aviation, via Wikimedia Commons)

A 2d BMW B-52G, deployed from Barksdale AFB, Louisiana, shortly after arriving at RAF Fairford, UK, on 25 May 1985 for exercise Busy Brewer. (Mike Freer – Touchdown Aviation, via Wikimedia Commons)

and RC-135s were also earmarked. SPF was first fully tested during exercise Busy Prairie, 22–25 September 1980. Fourteen 5th BMW B-52Hs deployed from Minot to Whiteman AFB (simulating a forward operating base), joined by EC/RC/KC-135s and U-2Rs. The B-52Hs conducted simulated combat operations over the Nellis Range Complex. Meanwhile, 319th BMW B-52Hs and 9th SRW SR-71As participated in the flying portion of the exercise from their home bases. On 23 November 1981, during Bright Star '82 (fiscal year 1982) eight SPF B-52Hs (four each from 5th and 319th BMW) conducted what was then SAC's longest training mission from their home bases, delivering conventional bombs on a simulated runway target in Egypt during a 31-hour, 15,000-mile mission. On 1 January 1983 United States Central Command (CENTCOM) activated, replacing RDJTF. From 1982 exercise Gallant Eagle was conducted, becoming the biennial CENTCOM Conventional Forces Exercise, centred on Fort Irwin, California. SAC routinely contributed aircraft to the exercise. Throughout the 1980s this exercise alternated with the, by now biennial, Middle East Bright Star exercises.

From 1988, following the B-1B's introduction, several B-52G units switched from a nuclear/conventional tasking to an exclusively conventional tasking, including maritime/sea surveillance missions, equipped with AGM-84 Harpoon anti-ship missiles and underwater mines, as well as conventional bombs for overland use.

A 2d ACCS, 55th SRW EC-135C, deployed from Offutt AFB, arriving at Biggs Army Air Field, El Paso, Texas, at the start of exercise Busy Prairie II. This was the second SAC exercise testing all aspects of the SPF, and took place during the week of 8 June 1981. Brigadier General John Shaud was aboard the aircraft. As 57th Air Division commander he also served as the SPF commander when directed by CINCSAC, a capacity he was acting in here. (NARA)

A 905th AREFS, 319th BMW, KC-135A deployed from Grand Forks AFB, rolls out on the runway after arriving at Biggs AAF for Busy Prairie II. (NARA)

Three 46th BMS, 319th BMW, B-52Hs from Grand Forks AFB, parked in a hot refuelling site at Biggs AAF during Busy Prairie II. Note the four fuel bladders in front of each aircraft, which allow refuelling facilities to be established at bare bases. Busy Prairie II was more extensive than the first Busy Prairie. Deployment was within 24 hours, to the bare base, desert environment at Biggs AAF. Night low-level missions began 36 hours after initiation and continued for five nights across the Nellis Range Complex and Utah Test and Training Range. (NARA)

A 2d ACCS, 55th SRW EC-135C and a 28th BMW B-52H at Biggs AAF during Busy Prairie II. Note the tent city to accommodate the deployed personnel. RDJTF staff participated in the SPF's tasking; CINCSAC would continue to maintain control over the SPF in a crisis, however, while the SPF is deployed to support the RDJTF, they could fall under the tactical command and control of the RDJTF Air Component Commander. This commander had the responsibility and authority to develop plans and direct the targeting and tasking of the SPF. (NARA)

A 46th BMS, 319th BMW, B-52H deploys its drag chute while landing at Biggs AAF during Busy Prairie II. This B-52H shows the standard camouflage scheme adopted by B-52s (apart from B-52Ds) from the late 1960s onwards, replacing the original silver schemes. Known as the 'SIOP Scheme', it consisted of FS 17875 white undersides and nose (intended to reflect nuclear flash), with FS 34201 tan, FS 34159 medium green and FS 34079 dark green upper sides. (NARA)

A 99th SRS, 9th SRW, U-2R, from Beale AFB, taxis out at Biggs AAF during Busy Prairie II. The truck following the U-2R carries the 'pogo crew' who will recover the two auxiliary 'pogo' underwing outrigger wheels that are jettisoned during the take-off run. (NARA)

A 5th BMW B-52H flies over the pyramids at Giza during exercise Bright Star '83 in Egypt. (NARA)

Left: A 5th BMW B-52H during Bright Star '83, operating from Cairo West AB, Egypt, for the exercise. (NARA)

Below: A 2d BMW KC-10A at Cairo West AB during Bright Star '83. Note the fuel bladder in the foreground. (NARA)

A 2d BMW KC-10A refuels a US Navy KA-6D of VA-65, which was operating from the USS *Dwight D Eisenhower* during Bright Star '83. While KC-135s required fitment of a Boom Drogue Adapter (BDA) to their flying boom to refuel probe-and-drogue receivers (which, when fitted, precluded it from refuelling receptacle-equipped receivers), the KC-10A featured an integral hose drogue unit in the rear fuselage to allow refuelling of both probe- and receptacle-equipped receivers during the same mission. (NARA)

In a secret programme launched in the aftermath of the 1986 US airstrikes on Libya, 105 AGM-86B ALCMs had their W80 thermonuclear warheads replaced by 2,000-lb high-explosive blast fragmentation warheads, becoming AGM-86C Conventional ALCMs (CALCMs); these gained initial operational capability (IOC) in January 1988, becoming fully operational in 1991.

Operational missions

SAC supported several 1980s operational missions:

Operation Eagle Claw, the abortive 1980 hostage rescue mission to Iran, saw KC-135s refuelling the rescue force's EC-130Es and MC-130Es.

Operation Urgent Fury, the 1983 Grenada invasion, saw KC-10s and KC-135s refuelling the numerous USAF aircraft involved. RC-135s undertook strategic reconnaissance.

B-52s were initially considered to make the 1986 Operation El Dorado Canyon attacks on Libya, before planners settled on United States Air Forces in Europe (USAFE) F-111Fs/EF-111As. The F-111F/EF-111A force required considerable air refuelling support, especially as it had to take the circuitous route around Continental Europe, having been denied overflight by those nations. A third of the KC-10 fleet (mostly 22d AREFW aircraft, others from 2d BMW and 68th AREFG) deployed to Mildenhall and Fairford, joining existing ETTF KC-135s. Seventeen KC-10s and eight KC-135s took part in the operation, some as air-spares, others refuelling the KC-10s that directly supported the F-111F/EF-111As. Each F-111F/EF-111A flight had a dedicated KC-10; one KC-10 also acted as the overall airborne mission command post. SAC RC-135s, SR-71As and U-2Rs undertook pre- and post-strike reconnaissance.

Operation Just Cause, the December 1989–January 1990 US intervention in Panama, saw KC-10s and KC-135s refuelling the MAC transports carrying personnel and equipment to Panama, and the escorting fighters. RC-135s provided reconnaissance support.

Exercises and Competitions

Between 8 and 16 July 1979, SAC conducted the first Global Shield exercise, a comprehensive, no-notice, nuclear war plan exercise; the command exercised every Emergency War Order (EWO) phase SIOP procedure short of nuclear warfare. Units generated hundreds of bombers, tankers, and missiles to alert status. Aircraft and personnel dispersed to preselected bases and flew sorties over radar bomb-scoring sites. Global Shield became annual, growing in scope and intensity. Global Shield '81 (26 January–16 February) was typical. Over 100,000 SAC personnel in the United States and Guam responded to a simulated Cold War escalation, dispersing over 120 bombers and tankers to thirty locations, improving SAC's ability to survive a surprise attack. Other unarmed bombers flew airborne alert missions on low-level routes over Colorado, New Mexico, Kansas, and Texas. SAC missile crews launched two Minuteman IIIs from Vandenberg AFB, California, over the Western Test Range toward Kwajalein Atoll. Immediately prior to the simulated attack on the US, around 100 SAC bombers and tankers conducted positive-control MITO launches from seventy locations. North American Aerospace Defense Command (NORAD) conducted concurrent air defence exercises in parallel to Global Shield, pitting US and Canadian fighters against SAC bombers.

The annual SAC Bombing and Navigation Competition ('Bomb Comp'), known as Giant Voice 1971–1987 (Proud Shield from 1988), at Barksdale AFB tested crew skills and equipment in a demanding environment. Royal Air Force (RAF) bomber crews competed from 1951, Tactical Air Command (TAC) F-111s from 1974, AFRES

Two LGM-30G Minuteman III ICBMs are launched twelve seconds apart at Vandenberg AFB during Global Shield '79. They headed over the Western Test Range to the missile range at Kwajalein Atoll. (NARA)

A simulated launch sequence takes place inside the 44th SMW's Launch Control Facility Trainer at Ellsworth AFB, during Global Shield '84. As would be the case for an operational Launch Control Center, two missile launch officers are present, although the second is obscured by the first here. The two missile launch officer stations were intentionally separated to prevent either being able to initiate a missile launch without the other, in accordance with the 'two-man rule'. After various checks to validate a launch order, both missile launch officers needed to turn their launch keys within 2 seconds of each other to initiate an ICBM launch; a second missile crew in a separate LCC was also required to 'vote' that the launch was valid to allow the launch to proceed. (NARA)

Four B28FI thermonuclear bombs, each with a yield of up to 1.45 mt, are loaded on a 28th BMW B-52H at Ellsworth AFB by 28th Munitions Maintenance Squadron personnel, during Global Shield '83. Other free-fall nuclear bombs were available to SAC. The huge 9-mt B53 bomb, based on the Titan II warhead, was intended for targeting deeply buried Soviet command centres and submarine pens. The B61 had yields varying between 0.3 and 340 kt, depending on model. Finally, the B83 had variable yields up to 1.2 mt. (NARA)

The bomb bay of a 28th BMW B-52H at Ellsworth AFB during Global Shield '84. It accommodates the standard strategic nuclear penetration war load of four B28FIs forward, and six AGM-69A SRAMs, with 170–200-kt-yield W69 warheads on a rotary launcher aft. The total load yield carried is up to around 466 times the destructive power of the Little Boy bomb dropped on Hiroshima. The AGM-131 SRAM II, in development to replace AGM-69A, was cancelled in 1991 after the Cold War's conclusion. (NARA)

Personnel in M17 masks and nuclear, biological and chemical (NBC) warfare gear conduct simulated decontamination of a 28th BMW B-52H at Ellsworth AFB during Global Shield '84. (NARA)

and ANG tankers from 1977 and 1978 respectively. The Fairchild Trophy was the top Bomb Comp award, made to the bomber/tanker unit compiling the highest bomber/tanker mission points.

Other awards were the **Bartsch Trophy** (for the B-52 unit attaining highest electronic countermeasures (ECM) points); **Crumm Trophy** (B-52, or until 1980 RAF Vulcan, unit with best high-altitude bombing score); **Doolittle Trophy** (numbered Air Force whose B-52 units attained best overall combined low-level bombing and SRAM accuracy scores); **Dougherty Trophy** (B-52 unit with best overall combined low-level bombing and SRAM accuracy scores); **Mathis Trophy** (unit with most high- and low-level bombing and time control points); **Meyer Trophy** (top F-111/FB-111, or from 1984 RAF Tornado, unit compiling most low-level bombing, time control and ECM

An honour guard stands at attention as 509th BMW personnel, participating in Giant Voice '87, disembark from a 509th AREFS KC-135A after arriving at Barksdale AFB for the symposium and awards banquet. The painted 'red carpet' leads to the event's host building. The KC-135A is in the standard overall FS 16473 gloss aircraft grey. The large cargo door gave the KC-135 a useful secondary cargo capability. (NARA)

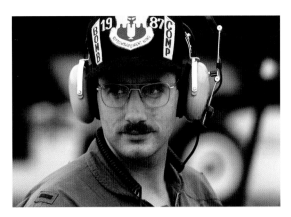

Right: A 43d BMW air crewman stands by during Giant Voice '87. (NARA)

Below: Jubilant 5th BMW personnel are awarded the Fairchild Trophy, as the overall winners of Proud Shield '88. Presenting the award is General John T. Chain, Jr, CINCSAC. (NARA)

points); **Navigation Trophy**, renamed Holloway Trophy from 1986 (top tanker unit in navigation); **Saunders Trophy** (top tanker unit); **LeMay Trophy**, awarded from 1980 replacing the former Bombing Trophy (bomber crew compiling the most points in high- and low-level bombing); **McDonnell-Douglas Trophy**, awarded from 1982, renamed Ellis KC-10 Trophy in 1986 (best KC-10A team); **Ryan Trophy**, presented from 1982 (B-52 unit with the best bombing score, resolving concerns over inequitable competition in bombing accuracy between B-52 units and those with more modern FB-111As); **Davis Trophy**, presented from 1984 (most improved unit compared to the previous year); **Mitchell Trophy**, presented from 1988 (bomber unit with top conventional bombing accuracy scores, ECM environment survival, and avoiding intercepting fighters) – B-1Bs, with their nuclear-only mission, could not compete for the **Mitchell Trophy**; the **Smith Trophy**, first awarded in 1989 (top scoring B-52 unit in gunnery and fighter defence).

Royal Australian Air Force (RAAF) F-111Cs first attended Giant Voice '80; they subsequently attended biennially. Giant Voice '81 saw no guest bomber participation; the RAF was converting from Vulcan to Tornado, and TAC and the RAAF did not attend. ANG/AFRES KC-135s did participate. Giant Voice '82 featured a format change: an initial phase (February to September) allowed participating units to evaluate their planning and execution of a series of missions, resulting in selection of the top two bomber and tanker crews. The final competition (1–8 November) decided the winning units. RAAF F-111Cs also returned. TAC F-111Ds attended Giant Voice '83. Giant Voice '84 saw RAF Tornados and USAFE F-111s attend for the first time; inert practice bombs were dropped on the Nellis Range for the first time during Phase One (all other scoring was electronic). Due to their more modern avionics, FB-111A wings enjoyed a distinct advantage over B-52 wings, taking every Fairchild Trophy from 1974 to 1984, except 1980. However, the new Offensive Avionics System (OAS) and ALCM made B-52s more competitive; a B-52 wing won the Fairchild Trophy in 1985 and in the subsequent years, until a B-1B unit won in 1989. TAC F-111s and RAF Tornados also participated. Giant Voice '86 saw no overseas participation, while 92d BMW B-52s dominated, taking nine trophies. Subsequently, the rules were changed to exclude aircraft specifically modified for the competition, while SAC Operations Staff (rather than wings) would henceforth select competing crews. Proud Shield '88 saw EC-135s and B-1Bs compete for the first time (EC-135s competed in the KC-135 phase as they retained in-flight refuelling capability), while F-111 crews could now compete for the Fairchild Trophy.

Ellsworth AFB hosted Giant Sword, SAC's Munitions Loading Competition (Combat Weapons Loading Competition from 1982), or 'Load Comp'. The top award was the Barrentine Trophy (Best Munitions Competition Team); other major awards were for Best Security Police Team, Best Munitions Load Crew, Best Crew Chief and Best Combined Load Crew. Giant Sword '84 first featured ALCMs in a competitive loading event. Giant Sword '86 moved to Fairchild AFB, returning to Ellsworth in 1987. Giant Sword '88 was cancelled due to funding restrictions. Giant Sword '89 (the final Load Comp and the first involving B-1B wings) returned to Fairchild.

A 'maintenance standardization and evaluation team' inspector observes as 509th BMW personnel load an inert training SRAM aboard an FB-111A during the Giant Sword '85 Combat Weapons Loading Competition at Ellsworth AFB. (NARA)

Above: A 92d BMW B-52G is
loaded with AGM-86Bs during
Giant Sword '85 at Ellsworth AFB.
(NARA)

Right: Personnel from the
509th BMW weapons load team
and security police team pose with
the Barrentine Trophy after winning
Giant Sword '85. (NARA)

Olympic Arena, SAC's Missile Competition, at Vandenberg AFB saw ICBM wings compete for the Blanchard Trophy for highest combined score. Other awards were Best Titan II Wing, Best Minuteman Wing, Best Missile Operations, Best Missile Civil Engineering Team, Best Missile Security Police Team, Best Missile Maintenance Team and Best Missile Communications Team.

SAC B-52 units had participated in RAF Strike Command's Bombing and Navigation Competition intermittently since 1958, known to SAC from 1967 as 'Giant Strike'. After missing the 1974 and 1975 competitions, SAC returned for Giant Strike VI in 1976 at RAF Marham where 320th BMW won the Blue Steel and Camrose Trophies. However, in the following years SAC failed to win major trophies. SAC's final attendance was Giant Strike XI in 1981; four crews competed, representing 5th, 319th (two crews) and 410th BMWs. Out of twenty-two competing crews, the SAC crews placed 13th, 15th, 19th and 22nd.

SAC Structure

SAC Wings were generally assigned to Air Divisions (ADs), which in turn were assigned to either 8th or 15th AF, or directly to SAC HQ. For clarity, due to periodic restructuring, wings will be described separately to the ADs and AFs to which they were assigned.

SAC Wings

Aircraft were pooled and shared by the squadrons in SAC wings, unlike other MAJCOMs where aircraft were generally assigned directly to the squadrons. Consequently, while aircraft often displayed wing markings, squadron markings were rare in SAC. Bomber/tanker squadron unit establishment varied from the equivalent of ten to eighteen aircraft, albeit with the proviso mentioned that the squadrons did not actually have their own allocation of aircraft. ICBM squadrons had fifty missiles, apart from Titan II squadrons with just nine each.

Bombardment wings generally included bomber and tanker squadrons. While it would have been more efficient, and less costly, to group larger numbers of bombers at certain bases and tankers at other bases, SAC chose instead to co-locate smaller numbers of bombers and tankers together, aiding force-survivability. As both were essential to achieving wartime mission objectives (the bombers could not reach their targets without tanker support), the destruction of, for example, a sizeable proportion of SAC's tankers, if grouped at one base, would have rendered a corresponding proportion of bombers useless, even if they survived elsewhere, hence the basing approach SAC took to mitigate against this.

The 2d Bombardment Wing, Heavy (BMW) at Barksdale AFB, Louisiana, was assigned 62d Bombardment Squadron, Heavy (BMS) and 596th BMS with B-52Gs. Some wing B-52Gs were modified to carry and launch ALCMs during the decade. From 1988 62d BMS gained a dedicated conventional mission, subsequently only flying the wing's non-ALCM modified B-52Gs, while 596th BMS only flew the ALCM-modified B-52Gs. The KC-135A-equipped 71st Air Refueling Squadron, Heavy (AREFS) and 913th AREFS were also initially assigned. Among the wing's KC-135As was 61-0316, configured as the 8th AF commander's VIP transport; this was destroyed on 19 March 1985 after its auxiliary power unit (APU) caught fire while ground refuelling at Cairo West Air Base (AB), Egypt. The 71st AREFS remained with the wing for the remainder of the decade with KC-135As; however, 913th AREFS inactivated on 1 November 1981, making room for the new KC-10 programme at Barksdale. Therefore, on the same date 32d AREFS was activated and assigned to 2d BMW with KC-10As. In 1987 it won the Spaatz Trophy for 'outstanding air refuelling unit'. In the late 1980s, KC-10A bases were reorganised with two approximately ten-aircraft-equivalent squadrons, instead of a single larger squadron. Consequently, 2d AREFS activated on 3 January 1989, thereafter sharing the pooled KC-10As with 32d AREFS. By 1989, 2d BMW was assigned thirty-seven B-52Gs (62d/596th BMS), fifteen KC-135As (71st AREFS), and nineteen KC-10As (2d/32d AREFS). Late in the decade the wing adopted fleur-de-lis markings on its B-52Gs, KC-135As and KC-10As; prior to that KC-135As had used yellow/green checkerboard fin-top markings. The 2d BMW was assigned to 19th AD, itself assigned to 8th AF, until 1 December 1982 when 2d BMW was reassigned to 42d AD (still under 8th AF). On 16 June 1988 2d BMW was reassigned directly to 8th AF.

A 2d BMW KC-135A landing at RAF Mildenhall, England, on 14 August 1985 while on TDY with 306th SW. (Mike Freer – Touchdown Aviation, via Wikimedia Commons)

A 2d BMW KC-10A, with its Advanced Aerial Refueling Boom extended, prepares to refuel 33d TFW F-15s from Eglin AFB, Florida, during exercise Ocean Venture '82. (NARA)

A minimum interval take-off (MITO) by 2d BMW B-52Gs from Barksdale AFB in 1986. The next B-52G is visible through the smoke left by the preceding aircraft. This MITO was being conducted under combat conditions during an operational readiness inspection (ORI) by the SAC Inspector General Team. (NARA)

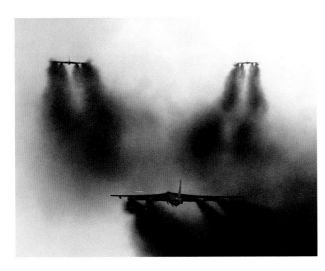

Three 2d BMW B-52Gs fan out on different headings after a MITO departure from Barksdale during the 1986 ORI. The thick smoke left behind is typical of J57-powered B-52 and KC-135 variants due to that engine's water-injection system. Water injection was intended for brief use, at temperatures above 20 °F (-6.7 °C), during take-off only. Demineralised water was injected into the inlet and diffuser section of each engine. This increased the density of inlet and combustion air, increasing thrust. By-products were unburned fuel leaving the exhaust, causing the characteristic dense black smoke as well as increased noise. (NARA)

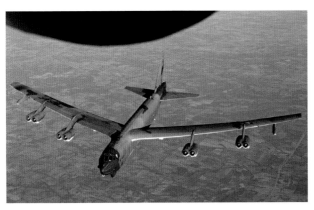

A 2d BMW B-52G, viewed from the boom operator's position in a KC-135, during the 1986 ORI. The white nose of the B-52's SIOP camouflage scheme was a potential visual give away to hostile interceptors when operating at low level. Therefore, throughout the 1980s, many SIOP-camouflaged B-52s progressively had their nose and cockpit sections repainted in FS 36081 dark grey, as seen on this B-52G, to make them less conspicuous. The extent of the repainted area varied. (NARA)

A B-52G and KC-10A of the 2d BMW at Barksdale during Proud Shield '88. The KC-10A is in the later FS 36081 dark grey and FS 16473 light grey camouflage scheme, nicknamed 'Shamu' after the killer whale. The B-52G is in the later toned-down green/grey 'Strategic Camouflage Scheme'. General Chain, who became CINCSAC on 22 June 1986, introduced a number of changes influenced by his Tactical Air Command background, which were not universally popular with personnel used to SAC's traditional rigid standards. These included colourful cloth nametags on flying suits, and the reintroduction of aircraft nose art, as seen here with *ACK-ACK ANNIE II*. The nose-art programme was seen as a successful morale booster, bringing air crews and crew chief closer together in selection of the artwork designs. (NARA)

The 5th BMW at Minot AFB, North Dakota, was assigned 23d BMS and 906th AREFS, operating B-52Hs and KC-135As respectively. In 1980 5th BMW became spearhead of the Strategic Projection Force, SAC's RDJTF contribution, with 23d BMS adding a Middle East conventional bombing contingency tasking to its strategic nuclear warfare mission. It completed transition to OAS modified aircraft in 1983. OAS replaced obsolete analogue bombing and navigation system with solid-state, off-the-shelf digital equipment compatible with ALCM and SRAM. The 906th AREFS won the 1984 and 1985 Spaatz Trophies. In 1985 5th BMW won the Omaha Trophy, awarded to 'the outstanding wing in SAC'. In 1988 5th BMW won the Fairchild Trophy. The wing received ALCMs in 1989. By 1989 the wing operated seventeen B-52Hs and thirteen KC-135As, gaining winged skull markings on both types. The KC-135As added the winged skull to existing markings of a tanker silhouette superimposed over a red sun on a white band. The 5th BMW was assigned to 57th AD (in turn assigned to 15th AF).

The 6th Strategic Wing (SW) at Eielson AFB, Alaska, was assigned 24th Strategic Reconnaissance Squadron (SRS). In the early 1980s it operated two RC-135S Cobra Ball Telemetry Intelligence (TELINT) aircraft (61-2663/61-2664), which, along with the land-based Cobra Dane radar at Shemya AFB and the sea-based Cobra Judy radar on board the USNS *Observation Island*, observed Soviet ICBM tests during re-entry and verified Soviet compliance with the Strategic Arms Limitation Treaty (SALT) and other treaties. Consequently 24th SRS maintained an RC-135S on 24-hour alert at

A 5th BMW KC-135A
deployed from Minot AFB
to RAF Mildenhall, England,
on TDY with the 306th SW,
seen on 30 March 1986. (Mike
Freer – Touchdown Aviation,
via Wikimedia Commons)

A 5th BMW B-52H under tow at Cairo West AB during Bright Star '83. B-52G and H models gained various distinctive 'warts' on their forward fuselage that they initially lacked. Under the nose are fairings for the AN/ASQ-151 Electro-Optical Viewing System (EVS), with AN/AAQ-6 forward-looking infrared (FLIR) to starboard and AN/AVQ-22 low-light level television camera (LLTV) to port – both are rotated closed here. EVS complimented the terrain avoidance system when flying at low level, especially useful in a wartime nuclear environment flying with cockpit thermal curtains closed. The pilot, co-pilot and both navigators had EVS displays, onto which radar and other flight data was overlaid. EVS could also be used for damage assessment. (NARA)

A 5th BMW B-52H landing at Cairo West AB during exercise Bright Star '83. (NARA)

Major Bill Weller, left, and First
Lieutenant Doug Morse, right, of the
23d BMS, 5th BMW, flying their B-52H
over Alaska at low level to evade radar.
This was during SAC exercise Giant
Warrior '89, during which their aircraft
was deployed to Eielson AFB. (NARA)

the forward operating location at Shemya AFB on tiny and remote Shemya in the Aleutian Islands, 1,600 miles (2,575 kilometres) from Eielson and only 500 miles (800 kilometres) from Kamchatka's east coast. Soviet ICBM/SLBM tests would launch from Plesetsk, Kapustin-Yar, Tyuratam (Baikonur) or Sary Shagan in the western/central USSR, or the Barents Sea/White Sea with their re-entry vehicles targeted at the Klyuchi test range on the Kamchatka Peninsula in the Soviet Far East. At Shemya the alert crew would launch on the sound of the klaxon, being in position off Kamchatka in time to record re-entry with the RC-135S's starboard-side optical sensors. RC-135S 61-2664 was written off after striking the embankment at the approach end of the runway while landing in challenging conditions at Shemya on 15 March 1981, tragically killing six crewmen. A replacement RC-135S (converted from C-135B 61-2662) was delivered to 6th SW on 11 November 1983. The tragic 31 August 1983 shoot down of a Korean Air Lines Boeing 747 near Sakhalin by a Soviet PVO (Air Defence Forces) Su-15 brought attention to 6th SW operations. The Soviets initially claimed they believed they were targeting an RC-135, resulting in calls from some quarters to curtail the supposedly 'provocative' RC-135 operations, especially Cobra Ball flights. Common sense prevailed and the latter continued. On 1 April 1988 6th SW was redesignated 6th Strategic Reconnaissance Wing (SRW). A single RC-135X Cobra Eye (62-4128) was delivered to 6th SW on 16 July 1989, considerably delayed from the originally intended April 1986 delivery due to protracted development. Cobra Eye was designed for midcourse optical tracking and identification of ICBM/SLBM re-entry vehicles via a long-wave infrared telescope. It operated in conjunction with the DoD's Strategic Defense Initiative Organization (SDIO). The first operational Cobra Eye mission occurred on 15 August 1989. Cobra Eye also supported US ICBM/SLBM tests. The Cold War's end, the redundancy of its mission, and curtailment of SDI projects meant that Cobra Eye had a short operational life; in the post-Cold War years it was converted into a third RC-135S. The 24th SRS received one-off RC-135T 55-3121 on 12 December 1979, a former Electronic Intelligence (ELINT) aircraft, but used by 24th SRS as a cockpit trainer for RC-135S crews. In 1982 the RC-135T's J57-P/F-43Ws were replaced by TF33-PW-102 thrust-reversing turbofans, allowing for more useful training as the RC-135S featured thrust reversing TF33-P5s (not all TF33 turbofan models featured thrust reversers). NKC-135A 55-3129 was temporarily assigned to 24th SRS as a trainer (3 January–7 April 1982) while the RC-135T was being re-engined. It was originally planned that the RC-135T would be transferred to 55th SRW as a trainer, after being replaced by dedicated TC-135S trainer 62-4133. However, before the transfer occurred, the RC-135T tragically crashed into a mountain near Valdez Airport, Alaska, while conducting practice approaches on 25 February 1985; all three crew members were killed. The TC-135S was delivered to 24th SRS on 22 July 1985. The 6th SW/SRW also operated Alaskan Tanker Task Force (ATTF) missions with temporary duty (TDY) SAC, ANG and AFRES KC-135s. The 6th SW won the 1983 P. T. Cullen Award for contributing most to SAC's intelligence collection efforts. The wing was assigned to 47th AD (under 15th AF), being reassigned to 14th AD (also under 15th AF) on 1 October 1985.

The 7th BMW at Carswell AFB, Texas, was assigned 9th BMS, 20th BMS and 4018th Combat Crew Training Squadron (CCTS) with B-52Ds. On 1 October 1982 9th BMS re-equipped with B-52Hs (deliveries had commenced in May), 20th BMS following suit by 30 September 1983; these were former 93d BMW/Castle and 28th BMW/Ellsworth B-52Hs. The 4018th CCTS inactivated on 31 March 1983 due to the withdrawal of B-52Ds from USAF service. As was usual, 7th BMW's B-52s were pooled, apart from between 1 October 1982 and 30 September 1983, after 9th BMS had re-equipped with B-52Hs, while 20th BMS continued to fly B-52Ds. In 1986 9th BMS gained ALCMs. The 7th AREFS was assigned with KC-135As. These introduced yellow/black diamond markings; from 1987 KC-135A markings changed to the Fort Worth city flag with 'FORT WORTH' and 'TEXAS' titles. By 1989 7th BMW operated thirty-five B-52Hs and twenty-six KC-135As. The wing was assigned to 19th AD (itself assigned to 8th AF). On 13 June 1988 7th BMW was reassigned directly to 8th AF.

A 7th BMW B-52D seen deployed to Fairford on 25 October 1981 during exercise 'Busy Brewer'. B-52Ds adopted unique camouflage; when modified for service in Vietnam they also received the South East Asia (SEA) camouflage scheme. SEA camouflage used the same upper three colours as the SIOP camouflage used by other B-52s, but with undersides and sides in FS 17038 gloss black. (Mike Freer – Touchdown Aviation, via Wikimedia Commons)

A 7th AREFS, 7th BMW, KC-135A landing at Mildenhall on 30 December 1985, while on TDY with the 306th SW. (Mike Freer – Touchdown Aviation, via Wikimedia Commons)

The 9th SRW at Beale AFB, California, was assigned 1st SRS with SR-71s and 99th SRS with U-2s. The 4029th Strategic Reconnaissance Training Squadron (SRTS) activated on 1 August 1981, conducting SR-71 and U-2 pilot training; previously pilot training was conducted by the operational squadrons. Activation of 4029th SRTS was partly driven by increased pilot demand with the U-2R/TR-1A re-entering production. On 1 July 1986 4029th SRTS was replaced by 5th SRTS (four-digit units were temporary MAJCOM units, unentitled to a unit history or heritage, unlike permanent 'AFCON' – Air Force Controlled – units). 5th SRTS retained the U-2/TR-1 training mission, but passed SR-71 training back to 1st SRS. The 9th SRW held fourteen operational SR-71As and a single SR-71B trainer in 1980, although of those only eight 'Primary Authorised Aircraft' were in use at any one time (the remainder in storage). One SR-71A was withdrawn in 1987 and another crashed into the South China Sea in 1989. In 1980 seven of the original production U-2Rs were still assigned, two of which crashed in Korea during the decade (on 5 October 1980 and 22 May 1984). An additional U-2R was transferred from flight test to 9th SRW in 1981. U-2 training was initially provided by a pair of U-2CTs, which retired in 1987. When the U-2R/TR-1A re-entered production, some joined 9th SRW, while others were assigned to 17th RW in the UK (q.v.). Of the new production, seven were completed as U-2Rs (funded from 'black budgets'), all being assigned to 9th SRW as they were completed (between 1983 and 1989), although the first new production U-2R was transferred out of 9th SRW (and SAC) between 1985 and 1988 for flight test. The remaining twenty-four new-production single-seaters were completed as TR-1As; twelve were delivered upon completion (between 1981 and 1989) to 9th SRW (the remainder going to 17th RW or flight test). Of these twelve 9th SRW TR-1As, one was transferred to flight test at Palmdale in 1989 and four were subsequently transferred to 17th RW (three in 1983, one in 1987). In return three 17th RW TR-1As were transferred to 9th SRW, one in 1984 (which crashed at Beale on 18 July 1984, four months after reassignment to 9th SRW), the other two in 1988–89. New-production two-seaters were three TR-1Bs, two of which were delivered to 9th SRW in 1983 (the final one going to 17th RW in 1988) and a single TU-2R, delivered to 9th SRW in March 1988. Around fourteen T-38As were also assigned to the wing, originally as SR-71 crew companion trainers, later also used by U-2/TR-1 and KC-135Q crews for additional flight experience. Although used by crews from across the wing, 4029th/5th SRTS was primarily responsible for the T-38As. While U-2 operations expanded throughout the 1980s, SR-71 operations were suspended on 1 October 1989 (apart from proficiency training) and operations were terminated on 22 November 1989 following the decision to axe the SR-71 budget. On 15 March 1983 349th and 350th AREFS were reassigned to 9th SRW from the inactivating 100th AREFW (q.v.). These two squadrons shared KC-135Qs (thirty-eight by 1989) primarily supporting the SR-71s, but able to support other types too. The 9th SRW maintained a number of detachments worldwide. Det 1, 9th SRW at Kadena AB, Okinawa, Japan, operated a pair of SR-71As, reduced to a single SR-71A on 12 August 1988, which finally returned to Beale on 21 January 1990 as Det 1 drew down. Det 2, 9th SRW at Osan AB, Republic of Korea, operated the U-2R. Until September 1980 the U-2R detachment at RAF Akrotiri, Cyprus, was designated OL-OH (Operating Location-Olive Harvest), thereafter becoming Det 3, 9th SRW (usually with two U-2Rs). Det 4, 9th SRW at RAF Mildenhall, UK, was established on 31 March 1979 with one U-2R in the Creek Spectre SIGINT role; previously only TDY U-2 deployments had been made. Det 4 also supported periodic

SR-71A deployments – the UK Government stipulating early SR-71 deployments be no longer than twenty days, each sortie requiring UK permission. In February 1983 Det 4 ceased U-2R operations after 17th RW became operational with the TR-1A. In 1984 Prime Minister Thatcher agreed that Det 4 would become a permanent two-aircraft SR-71A detachment. It flew its last SR-71A sortie (a functional check flight) on 20 November 1989 (the two aircraft departing for Beale on 18/19 January 1990). Det 5, 9th SRW at Eielson AFB, Alaska, operated the SR-71A during 1979-80, conducting operational missions and cold weather tests. In January 1982 OL-OF (Operating Location-Olympic Flare) was established with the U-2R at Patrick AFB, Florida; in January 1983 this became the new Det 5, 9th SRW. Det 8, 9th SRW at Diego Garcia briefly conducted SR-71A operational missions in 1978–79. OL-Bodø at Bodø AB, Norway, was not an aircraft detachment, but an emergency recovery base for European SR-71 fights. The 9th SRW won the 1980 and 1985 P. T. Cullen Awards. Throughout the 1980s 9th SRW was assigned to 14th AD (under 15th AF).

Above: A 9th SRW SR-71A takes off from Beale AFB in 1982. (NARA)

Left: An SR-71A drops back from its KC-135Q tanker after refuelling in 1988. (NARA)

Below: A 9th SRW SR-71A prepares for a mission in 1984. (NARA)

Staff Sergeant Rex C. Brunelli, an ELINT operations specialist with Det 4, 9th SRW, processes data in the detachment's ELINT analysis van at Mildenhall in 1988. (NARA)

Right: The 9th SRW's SR-71B trainer, 17956, seen in flight during 1984. (NARA)

Below: TR-1A 80-1074 seen in flight near San Francisco in 1985. This aircraft had been delivered to the 9th SRW in February 1984. (NARA)

TR-1B 80-1065 of the 9th SRW approaching RAF Alconbury, England, on 28 October 1987 while deployed from Beale AFB. The following year Alconbury's 17th RW received its own TR-1B trainer. (Mike Freer – Touchdown Aviation, via Wikimedia Commons)

The KC-135Q was intended to refuel the SR-71 with its special JP-7 fuel. Consequently, the KC-135Q carried both standard JP-4 for its own use, usually in the wing tanks, and JP-7 for offloading to SR-71s, usually in the body tanks. The KC-135Q could burn JP-7 fuel in an emergency, although not routinely. The KC-135Q could also have its tanks flushed and fill all tanks with standard JP-4 for offload to receivers other than SR-71s. This was regularly done, as seen here. This 9th SRW KC-135Q, flown by a 350th AREFS crew, refuels a pair of 37th TFW F-4Gs from George AFB, CA, during 1988. The KC-135Q has finished refuelling the furthest F-4G, which is in 37th TFW wing commander's markings, while the nearest F-4G, in 561st TFS squadron commander's markings, will move across and refuel next. (NARA)

The 11th Strategic Group (SG) at RAF Fairford formed half of the European Tanker Task Force (ETTF), with 306th SW at RAF Mildenhall making up the remainder (q.v.). The 11th SG usually supported around fifteen TDY tankers (SAC, AFRES or ANG). The 11th SG maintained a detachment with a TDY KC-135 at Naval Air Station (NAS) Keflavik, Iceland, supporting the TAC/57th FIS air defence F-4Es, later F-15C/Ds, based there. Further 11th SG detachments were made to Riyadh (Saudi Arabia), Lajes Field (Azores) and NAS Sigonella (Sicily). Each of these forward detachments normally involved a couple of aircraft. In the early 1980s the 11th SG Keflavik Det became Det 1, 306th SW. On 1 October 1986 34th Strategic Squadron (SS) at Zaragoza AB, Spain, with TDY KC-10As, was reassigned to 11th SG from 306th SW. The 11th SG was assigned to 7th AD (7th AD in turn was assigned directly to SAC, until reassigned to 8th AF from 31 January 1982).

The 17th Reconnaissance Wing (RW) at RAF Alconbury, UK, and its assigned 95th Reconnaissance Squadron (RS) both activated on 1 October 1982 with high-altitude tactical reconnaissance responsibilities, supporting NATO and USAFE (uniquely under peacetime USAFE control, and wartime NATO control). It received its first TR-1A on 12 February 1983, slowly building up its fleet. Along with tactical recon, it took on the Creek Spectre strategic SIGINT mission, allowing Det 4, 9th SRW to cease U-2R operations in February 1983. As well as existing strategic recon systems, new sensor systems were developed. A key TR-1A tactical recon system was ASARS-2, introduced from 1985. Similar to the SR-71's ASARS-1, ASARS-2's antenna was located in a distinctive long nose. This finally provided tactical commanders with timely intelligence round the clock, irrespective of weather or light. The TR-1A's sensors were linked real time via datalink to the trailer-based TREDS (TR-1 Exploitation Demonstration System – codenamed Metro Tango) ground station at Hahn AB. The end of the Cold War came before the definitive (underground/hardened) TRIGS (TR-1 Ground Stations) were fielded. By late 1989 95th RS had eleven TR-1As and one TR-1B.

The 19th BMW at Robins AFB, Georgia, was assigned 28th BMS (with B-52Gs) and 912th AREFS (with KC-135As). The 28th BMS inactivated on 1 October 1983, passing most of its B-52Gs on to 43d SW at Andersen AFB – (The 28th BMS would reactivate on 1 July 1987, assigned to 384th BMW at McConnell AFB – q.v.) The 19th BMW won the 1981 Omaha Trophy. On 15 September 1982, a 19th BMW B-52G, commanded by Captain Robert L. Cavendish, lost both rudder elevator hydraulic systems during a training mission, severely crippling it. After considering all factors, Captain Cavendish decided to try to land the aircraft; no such landing had ever been attempted before. Having successfully landed their crippled B-52G, under almost impossible conditions, saving their lives and aircraft, Captain Cavendish's crew was awarded the 1982 Mackay Trophy, awarded annually for the most meritorious USAF

A 'Shamu' camouflaged KC-10A on TDY with the 34th SS at Zaragoza AB, Spain, in 1987, by which time 34th SS was assigned to 11th SG. Also posing for the photograph are a 50th TFW F-16C in wing commander's markings (from Hahn AB, West Germany), a 92d TFS, 81st TFW, A-10A (from RAF Bentwaters, England) and a 53d TFS, 36th TFW, F-15C (from Bitburg AB, West Germany); these USAFE jets were visiting Zaragoza for training. (NARA)

A 95th RS, 17th RW, TR-1A visiting RAF Upper Heyford from its base at RAF Alconbury on 23 June 1989. It has the elongated nose carrying ASARS-2 (Advanced Synthetic Aperture Radar System), the key reconnaissance system for the TR-1A. Its radar antennas looked out 100 miles to either side of the aircraft, producing extremely high-resolution, photograph-like images at long range; its sensors were linked, real-time, via datalink to ground stations. TR-1As provided tactical commanders with timely intelligence round the clock, irrespective of weather or light. In wartime the 95th RS would have maintained two TR-1As in continual orbit over Central Europe, requiring six TR-1As to be launched per day. (Mike Freer – Touchdown Aviation, via Wikimedia Commons)

flight. On 1 October 1983 19th BMW was redesignated 19th AREFW. On the same date 28th BMS inactivated and 99th AREFS activated and was assigned to the wing. Thereafter, 99th and 912th AREFS shared pooled KC-135As, upgraded to KC-135Rs from 1985 (operating twenty-five by late 1989). The wing adopted large yellow/blue checkerboard fin markings, sometimes with a black knight's helmet; later in the decade this was replaced by a Georgia map and sword, on a white stripe, retaining the black knight's helmet. The 912th AREFS also operated two unique ABNCPs on behalf of CENTCOM: the EC-135Y (converted from an NKC-135A in 1983, retaining the refuelling boom) and the EC-135N (converted from an ARIA C-135N in 1985, lacking a refuelling boom). In 1986 both received TF33-PW-102s, replacing their J57s, and received in-flight refuelling receptacles. The non-SAC, CENTCOM-supporting, EC-135N/Y mission was entirely unrelated to the usual SAC EC-135A/C/G/L mission; they were assigned to 912th AREFS purely for convenience of operation. The 19th BMW/AREFW was assigned to 42d AD (under 8th AF); on 16 June 1988 19th AREFW was reassigned to 8th AF.

The 22d BMW at March AFB, California, was assigned 2d BMS (with B-52Ds) and 22d AREFS (with KC-135As). On 1 October 1982 22d BMW was redesignated 22d AREFW. On the same date the B-52D-equipped 2d BMS inactivated (the only post-Vietnam B-52D unit to inactivate rather than convert to B-52G/Hs) and 9th AREFS (a former 100th AREFW KC-135Q unit) activated in its place with KC-10As, joining the existing 22d AREFS, which retained KC-135As. On 3 January 1989 6th AREFS activated, due to the reorganisation of KC-10A bases to have two such squadrons. Thereafter, 6th and 9th AREFS shared pooled KC-10As (twenty-two assigned by 1989). The 22d AREFS, which had operated seven KC-135As, inactivated on 1 December 1989 as part of the KC-10A build-up at March. Wing tail markings were green/white diamonds, with superimposed black mission bell on a yellow circle

Above: A line up of 19th AREFW KC-135Rs, deployed to Whiteman AFB from Robins AFB in 1989 for exercise Mighty Warrior '89. (NARA)

Right: A 22d AREFW KC-10A refuels a trio of F-4Ds of the 'Happy Hooligans', 178th FIS, 119th FIG, North Dakota ANG, in 1985. The KC-10A has the original finish of FS 17875 'Insignia White' and FS 16473 'Aircraft Gray', separated by a FS 15102 blue cheatline. (NARA)

A 22d AREFW KC-10A being refuelled by a KC-135E of the 117th AREFS, 190th AREFG, Kansas ANG, one of fourteen SAC-gained ANG KC-135 units. Both aircraft are in the FS 36081/FS 16473 'Shamu' scheme introduced late in the decade; when applied to KC-135s (replacing all over FS 16473 grey) it was nicknamed 'Baby Shamu'. (NARA)

for the KC-135s and the Army Air Force star on the KC-10s. The 22d BMW/AREFW was initially assigned to 12th AD (under 15th AF); on 1 October 1985 22d AREFW was reassigned to 47th AD (under 15th AF); further reassigned to 14th AD (under 15th AF) on 23 January 1987. Finally, on 1 July 1988 22d AREFW was assigned directly to 15th AF.

The 28th BMW at Ellsworth AFB, South Dakota, was assigned 37th BMS and 77th BMS with B-52Hs, 28th AREFS with KC-135As and 4th Airborne Command and Control Squadron (ACCS) with EC-135A/C/Gs. The 37th BMS inactivated on 1 October 1982. It reactivated with B-1Bs and was reassigned to 28th BMW on 1 January 1987. The 77th BMS remained active throughout, converting to B-1Bs during 1985–86 (the last B-52H departing on 11 March 1986). The wing's B-1Bs utilised nuclear gravity bombs and SRAMs. In 1989 28th BMW won the Omaha, Fairchild, Crumm and Eaker Trophies (best B-1B unit) while 77th BMS won the Ryan Trophy. The 28th AREFS converted from KC-135As to KC-135Rs during 1985. The 4th ACCS operated EC-135A/C/Gs ABNCPs, supporting 15th AF and SAC as part of PACCS, including conducting Airborne Launch Control System (ALCS) operations. If the Minuteman (and later Peacekeeper) ICBM Launch Control Centers (LCC) were destroyed or unable to receive launch orders, Airborne Launch Control Centers (ALCC, pronounced 'al-see') could launch the ICBMs via radio signals. EC-135A/C/Gs had ALCC facilities added in the late 1960s. Titan IIs could not be remotely launched via ALCS. Three dedicated 4th ACCS ALCCs (ALCCs Nos 1, 2 and 3) were on 24-hour ground alert, providing ALCS coverage for five of the six Minuteman (one later partially Peacekeeper-equipped) ICBM Strategic Missile Wings (SMWs). ALCCs were generally EC-135As; however, EC-135C/Gs could be substituted depending on availability. ALCC No. 1 was held on ground alert at Ellsworth, earmarked to launch and orbit between 44th SMW (Ellsworth) and 90th SMW (Francis E. Warren). ALCCs Nos 2 and 3 were held on ground alert forward deployed to Minot AFB. If launched, ALCC No. 2 would have orbited near 341st SMW (Malmstrom AFB), ALCC No. 3 between 91st SMW (Minot) and 321st SMWs (Grand Forks). From these three orbits they could provide ALCS assistance if required. Separately, 4th ACCS also maintained an EC-135C/G on ground alert at Ellsworth to act as the West Auxiliary Airborne Command Post (WESTAUXCP). WESTAUXCP was a backup to SAC's Looking Glass ABNCP, as well as a radio relay link between Looking Glass and ALCCs when airborne. Although ALCS-equipped, WESTAUXCP it did not have a dedicated ALCS mission. The 4th ACCS also flew some Looking Glass missions, supporting the primary 55th SRW efforts (q.v.). The 28th BMW's KC/EC-135s adopted blue/yellow tail stripe markings with a wavy border; these were replaced in the late 1980s by a depiction of the Mount Rushmore monument with 'Ellsworth' titles. By 1989, 28th BMW operated thirty-two B-1Bs, fifteen KC-135Rs and five/six/three/one EC-135A/C/G/ Ls. The 4th ACCS previously used 28th AREFS KC-135As as cockpit crew trainers for its J57 turbojet-powered EC-135A/C/G/Ls. When 28th AREFS converted to re-engined KC-135Rs these were unsuitable, so from 1989 KC-135A 61-0288 (a former EC-135L) was assigned to 28th BMW, used by 4th ACCS as a J57-powered trainer. The 28th BMW was assigned to 4th AD (under 15th AF); it was reassigned to 57th AD (15th AF) on 1 May 1982, returned to 4th AD on 23 January 1987, and reassigned to 12th AD on 15 July 1988 (12th AD was under 15th AF, until being reassigned to 8th AF on 1 July 1989).

B-52H 61-0003 of the 28th BMW from Ellsworth AFB, seen shortly after arriving at RAF Marham, England, on 5 June 1979 for RAF Strike Command's Bombing and Navigation Competition. The deployment of four B-52Hs (two from the 28th BMW, one each from the 319th and 410th BMWs) to this competition was named Giant Strike IX. No trophies were won by SAC's participants during the competition, which took place on 20–28 June. (Mike Freer – Touchdown Aviation, via Wikimedia Commons)

Ground crew chock the wheels of 28th BMW B-52H 61-0025 just after its arrival at Andersen AFB, Guam, for a stop-off while deploying from Ellsworth to Darwin, Australia, for exercise Glad Customer '82. (NARA)

A cockpit view as a 37th BMS crew fly their 28th BMW B-52H from Andersen AFB, Guam, to RAAF Base Darwin, Northern Territory, Australia, for Glad Customer '82. Notable features are the eight throttles, on which the aircraft commander's hand rests, while the co-pilot's EVS display is prominent. (NARA)

A line up of 28th BMW B-52Hs at Ellsworth during Global Shield '83. It is notable that the white paint of the SIOP camouflage scheme did not take as well to the nose radome material as to the rest of the fuselage, often discolouring to a tan colour as seen on all but the second aircraft here, the latter more recently repainted. As well as the EVS fairings under the nose, there are blisters on either side of the nose for an ALQ-117 radar warning antenna and on the radome top for an ALT-28 ECM antenna. (NARA)

Left: Airman first class William Haase of the 44th Security Police Squadron, guards 28th BMW B-52Hs on Ellsworth's flight line during Global Shield '83. (NARA)

Below: A 28th BMW B-52H during Bright Star '85 in Egypt; the aircraft was based at Cairo West AB for the duration. (NARA)

A 28th BMW B-1B over Ellsworth AFB during 1988. It is in the Strategic Camouflage Scheme of FS 34086 green drab/FS 36081 dark grey upper sides and FS 36081 dark grey/FS 36118 medium grey undersides. (NARA)

Right: A KC-135R refuels a B-1B, both from the 28th BMW, during 1988. (NARA)

Below: A 28th BMW KC-135A takes off from Ellsworth during Global Shield '84. During the 1980s most KC-135s were painted in overall FS 16473 gloss aircraft grey (a scheme introduced in the 1970s); however, some KC-135s still retained the former 1960s finish of overall FS 17178 silver/aluminium, as seen here. (NARA)

A 28th BMW KC-135R in 1988 in overall FS 16473 gloss aircraft grey. From 1983 the tail-mounted floodlight (TMF) was retrofitted to KC-135s and EC-135s, located in the protrusion at the top trailing edge of the vertical stabiliser. Nicknamed 'the streetlight', it was intended to ease night refuelling for boom operators, especially important as USAF aircraft increasingly adopted low-visibility colour schemes. The boom operator could control the light's intensity to minimise glare for the receiver pilots. (NARA)

Left: A female first lieutenant of the 28th AREFS, 28th BMW, at the controls of a KC-135R during a refuelling sortie over the North Sea during 1988, while on TDY with the ETTF. Although the USAF had accepted females as pilots since the late 1970s, they were barred from flying combat aircraft, including SAC's bombers. This was overturned in the early 1990s, opening all flying positions to women. (NARA)

Below: EC-135G 63-7994 of the 4th ACCS, 28th BMW, visiting Vandenberg during 1987. (NARA)

On board a 4th ACCS, 28th BMW, EC-135G during 1987. The positions in the right foreground are those for Common ALCS. (NARA)

EC-135G 62-3579 of the 4th ACCS, 28th BMW, over Ellsworth during 1988. EC-135s and RC-135s adopted a finish of FS 17875 insignia white and FS 16473 aircraft grey, separated by a FS 17038 black cheatline. (NARA)

EC-135C 62-3582 and crew of the 4th ACCS, 28th BMW, pose during 1987. The trailing wire antenna fairing can be seen on the EC-135C's underside. (NARA)

The 42d BMW at Loring AFB, Maine, was assigned B-52G-equiped 69th BMS, and KC-135A-equipped 42d and 407th AREFS (converting to KC-135Rs at decade's end). On 5 September 1983 a 42d AREFS KC-135A, commanded by Captain Robert J. Goodman, was deploying to the ETTF while 'dragging' a flight of 4th TFW F-4Es, also deploying to Europe. One F-4E lost an engine and suffered partial hydraulics failure. Having lost almost 20,000 feet, the F-4E crew jettisoned their external tanks to maintain speed and altitude, while diverting to Gander, Newfoundland, 500 miles away. Goodman's KC-135A escorted, refuelled and towed the crippled Phantom, which dropped to just 2,000 feet above the frigid ocean; four difficult hookups, all interrupted by disconnects, allowed the F-4E to reach Gander without mishap. Captain Goodman's crew was awarded the 1983 Mackay Trophy. The 42d BMW also received the 1983 Spaatz Trophy. In 1988 69th BMS adopted a dedicated conventional role with its B-52Gs, particularly focusing on maritime missions in the Atlantic, including sea surveillance; they were equipped with AGM-84 Harpoon anti-ship missiles and underwater mines, as well as conventional bombs. In the late 1980s the wing's B-52Gs gained tail markings of a moose-head on either a Maine map outline or carrying a bomb, sometimes with 'LORING' titles, plus 'LORING' on the underwing fuel tanks. The wing's KC-135As initially adopted blue/yellow diagonal fin-top stripes from around 1987, changing to variations of moose-head on Maine map or carrying a bomb, along with 'LORING' titles. By 1989 the wing held fifteen B-52Gs, twenty-four KC-135As and five KC-135Rs. The 42d BMW was assigned to 45th AD (under 8th AF) until being assigned directly to 8th AF on 29 March 1989.

The 43d SW at Andersen AFB, Guam, was assigned B-52D-equipped 60th BMS. Along with Carswell's 20th BMS/7th BMW, 60th BMS was the last unit to retire B-52Ds, replaced by 1 October 1983 with B-52Gs, deliveries of which had

Left: Captain Michael F. O'Neill, 69th BMS Chaplain, in front of a 42d BMW B-52G prior to a mission in 1983. Captain O'Neill logged more than 200 hours of flying time during his assignment at Loring AFB. (NARA)

Below: The crew of a 42d BMW B-52G deployed from Loring AFB to March AFB in front of their aircraft in 1988. They were there for Fifteenth Air Force's first 'Shootout' conventional bombing competition, in which they would shortly test their skills. (NARA)

commenced in May (former 19th BMW/Robins B-52Gs). From 1988 60th BMS had an exclusively conventional tasking, including Pacific maritime missions. The unit's B-52Gs briefly used fire-breathing dragon markings, later a palm tree. The 43d SW also handled TDY KC-135s, until 65th SS was activated and assigned to 43rd SW on 1 July 1986; thereafter it handled TDY tankers and bombers deployed to Andersen. On 4 November 1986 43rd SW became 43d BMW. The 43rd SW/BMW was assigned to 3d AD (3d AD was directly assigned to SAC, until 31 January 1982 when it was reassigned to 15th AF).

A 42d BMW KC-135A, in overall FS 17178 silver/aluminium, refuels a MAC C-141B during exercise Ocean Venture '81. This was primarily a naval exercise involving 120,000 service personnel, 250 ships, over 1,000 aircraft and fifteen nations. Various phases of the exercise took place in the South Atlantic, the Caribbean, the Atlantic off the Virginia Capes, the North Atlantic and the Baltic. Seen during the Caribbean phase, the C-141B is one of several on their way to paradrop US Army Rangers from the 2nd Battalion, 75th Infantry, over a drop zone in Puerto Rico. (NARA)

Two 43d SW B-52Ds off the South Korean coast during exercise Team Spirit '82. The nearest aircraft drops a training version of the Mk 52 1,000-lb underwater mine. (NARA)

Above: A 43d SW B-52D viewed from a KC-135A during exercise Team Spirit '82. (NARA)

Left: A 43d SW B-52G off Chinhae port, near Pusan, during the MINEX mine countermeasures (MCM) exercise that formed part of the joint US/ South Korean Exercise Team Spirit '84. (NARA)

Below: A 43d SW B-52G taking off from Andersen AFB during Theater Force Employment Exercise IV in 1985. (NARA)

Right: Personnel of the 43rd Munitions Maintenance Squadron prepare to load Mk 52 training mines onto a 43d SW B-52G at Andersen AFB during Team Spirit '85. (NARA)

Below: A 43d SW B-52G takes off from Andersen AFB for an aerial mining mission near South Korea during Team Spirit '85. (NARA)

Above: A 43d SW B-52G drops a Mk 52 training mine off Yeosu, South Korea, during Team Spirit '85. (NARA)

Right: A 43d BMW B-52G, carrying an AGM-84A Harpoon anti-ship missile, viewed from a KC-135 boom operator's position during 1989. (NARA)

The 44th SMW at Ellsworth AFB was assigned 66th, 67th and 68th Strategic Missile Squadrons (SMS), each with fifty silo-based LGM-30F Minuteman II ICBMs. Silos were east (66th SMS), north-east (67th SMS) and north-west (68th SMS) of Ellsworth. As was standard for Minuteman squadrons (and later the single Peacekeeper squadron at Francis E. Warren AFB), each squadron was split into five flights. Each flight had a Launch Control Facility (LCF), consisting of a hardened underground Launch Control Center (LCC), an above-ground Launch Control Support Building and ten Launch Facilities (LFs – ICBM silos). The LCF and LFs were dispersed several miles apart. Around a dozen officers and airmen were assigned to the LCF. The underground LCC, containing the command and control equipment for missile operations, was staffed 24 hours a day by two missile launch officers who had primary control over the flight's ten LFs containing the ICBMs. Each of the squadron's five LCCs had the ability to monitor and command all fifty of the squadron's LFs/ICBMs. Therefore, if an LCC was disabled, another LCC within the squadron would take control of its ten LFs/ICBMs. As noted previously, if all of the squadron LCCs were destroyed or unable to receive launch orders, the airborne EC-135s could instead launch the ICBMs through their ALCC facilities. The LF silos were unmanned, except when maintenance and security personnel were required. Each flight was designated with a letter. Within 44th SMW, 66th SMS controlled A through E Flights, 67th SMS controlled F through J Flights and 68th SMS controlled K through O Flights. Within the flight the LCF was designated 01, while the ten LF silos were designated 02 through 11. Therefore, within A Flight of 66th SMS, the LCF was A-01, while the ten LF silos were A-02 through A-11. The wing won the Blanchard Trophy, the top award at SAC's 1982 Missile Competition. The 44th SMW was assigned to 4th AD (under 15th AF), being reassigned to 57th AD (15th AF) on 1 May 1982, reassigned back to 4th AD on 23 January 1987 and further reassigned on 15 July 1988 to 12th AD (which was under 15th AF, until reassigned to 8th AF on 1 July 1989).

The 55th SRW at Offutt AFB, Nebraska, was assigned 1st ACCS, 2d ACCS, 38th SRS and 343d SRS. The 1st ACCS operated E-4 Advanced Airborne Command Posts (AABNCP) for the 'Nightwatch' National Emergency Airborne Command Post (NEACP, pronounced 'kneecap') mission; initially three E-4As and a single, much improved, E-4B. The E-4 was originally intended to replace both EC-135Js in the Nightwatch NEACP mission and EC-135Cs in the Looking Glass primary ABNCP mission. The three E-4As replaced the EC-135Js in the Nightwatch mission by the mid-1970s; E-4As accommodated the mission suites removed from the EC-135J that they replaced, while offering increased space and flight duration. The initial E-4B was intended to be the first of a fleet to replace EC-135Cs in the Looking Glass mission. The E-4B was equipped with back-end gear removed from an EC-135C, provided with nuclear thermal shielding and hardened against EMP. The E-4B added satellite communications to the existing low frequency/very low frequency (LF/VLF) radios. In the event the decision to replace EC-135Cs with E-4Bs was reversed; EC-135Cs retained the Looking Glass mission and further E-4B production was halted. The E-4B was briefly able to handle both Nightwatch, Looking Glass and ALCC missions. The E-4B flew its first Looking Glass mission on 4 March 1980 and used its ALCC capability to test launch a Minuteman ICBM on 1 April 1981. ALCC equipment was removed a short time later and the Looking Glass mission relinquished; thereafter the E-4 concentrated on the Nightwatch NEACP mission. Despite this, the E-4As were upgraded to E-4B standard by January 1985. One E-4 was maintained on forward-deployed ground alert at Andrews AFB, Maryland, a short helicopter flight from the White House. The E-4's NEACP role was to carry the

E-4B 73-1676 operated by the 1st ACCS, 55th SRW, at Offutt in 1984. This had been the first E-4A delivered to the USAF in 1973. It had been upgraded to E-4B standard and returned to the 55th SRW on 1 August 1983. (NARA)

Right: A 55th SRW E-4B turning on to Offutt's runway in 1984. (NARA)

Below: E-4B 74-0787 refuelling from a 117th AREFS, 190th AREFG, Kansas ANG, KC-135E in 1988. This was the third E-4, and the last to be delivered as an E-4A. It was upgraded to E-4B standard and redelivered to the 55th SRW on 28 January 1985. The fourth and final E-4 (75-0125) was delivered as an E-4B from the outset. (NARA)

National Command Authority (NCA) and a battle staff during the opening hours or days of a general conflict. The NCA comprised, jointly, POTUS (as commander-in-chief) and the SecDef, or their successors, i.e. the vice president and the deputy secretary of defense (DepSecDef). E-4s could also link into commercial telephone and radio networks to broadcast emergency messages to the population. Intended to stay airborne for a week in wartime, maintained aloft by in-flight refuelling, flight duration was only limited by engine oil lubricants.

The 2d ACCS operated EC-135C ABNCPs. Their most notable mission was the permanently airborne Looking Glass EC-135C primary ABNCP, providing command and control of US nuclear forces in the event that ground-based command centres were rendered inoperable. An EC-135C Looking Glass would remain on station until its replacement arrived on station, taking over the relevant command and communications links. Looking Glass also conducted ALCC duties for the Minuteman ICBMs of 351st SMW (Whiteman). These continuous airborne alert missions ended on 24 July 1990 after twenty-nine years; thereafter Looking Glass was maintained on ground alert with occasional flights. While Looking Glass maintained its airborne vigil, two other 2d ACCS EC-135Cs were maintained on 15-minute ground alert at Offutt. One was the East Auxiliary Airborne Command Post (EASTAUXCP). Although ALCS-equipped, EASTAUXCP it did not have a dedicated ALCS mission. The other was for Commander-in-Chief SAC (CINCSAC) provided that there was sufficient time for him to arrive at the aircraft in the event of hostilities. The initial improved EC-135C COMMON/PACER LINK I went on alert in June 1987, introducing completely revised state-of-the-art systems, including Common ALCS, which allowed the airborne staff to manage both Minuteman and Peacekeeper ICBMs and remotely retarget Peacekeeper ICBMs. Considerable teething problems with PACER LINK were not resolved until 1991. SAC operated twelve EC-135Cs in 1980, rising to thirteen in 1984 when one temporarily loaned to Pacific Air Forces (PACAF) was returned. These were split between 2d ACCS/55th SRW and 4th ACCS/28th BMW, with respective totals fluctuating, although 2d ACCS generally operated at least half of them – often more. In 1989 2d ACCS operated around seven EC-135Cs.

Crew from the 2d ACCS, 55th SRW, boarding EC-135C 63-8052 at Offutt. (NARA)

Captain Tom Neiss, foreground, 2d ACCS airborne missile combat crew commander, and Captain John Rogers, deputy airborne missile combat crew commander from the 1850th Communications Squadron, practice turning the Common ALCS ICBM launch keys inside COMMON/PACER LINK I EC-135C 63-8052. The improved Common ALCS was introduced in 1987; it allowed crews to launch both Minuteman and Peacekeeper ICBMs, and remotely retarget Peacekeeper ICBMs. (NARA)

A close-up of Captain Neiss' ALCS console and launch key. Like their ground-based equivalents, the operations officer and communications officer both had to turn their keys within 2 seconds to initiate an ICBM launch. Prior to that the Airborne Emergency Action Officer (AEAO), the operations officer, the communications officer and the EC-135's aircraft commander all had to validate the launch order. The aircraft commander then activated a switch to his left in the cockpit to enable the ALCS equipment. (NARA)

The 38th and 343d SRS operated the RC-135s; 38th SRS provided cockpit crews, while 343d SRS provided the back-end crews. These crews operated 55th SRW's various assigned RC-135 variants. Seven of the eight RC-135V Rivet Joint Electronic Intelligence (ELINT) and Communications Intelligence (COMINT) aircraft were converted from SAC's original RC-135Cs, while the eighth was converted from a surplus RC-135U; all were in service by 1977. The six COMINT RC-135Ms were converted from C-135Bs for use during the conflict in South East Asia, allowing SAC's RC-135Cs to continue focussing on their ELINT/COMINT duties against the Soviet Union, China and North Korea. At the conclusion of the war in South East Asia, the RC-135Ms flew 'Rivet Card' sorties from Hellenikon (Greece) and Kadena, but rarely to northern Europe where their COMINT role was not particularly useful (ELINT being the prime mission there). From 1978 the RC-135Ms were converted to RC-135W Rivet Joint standard, with the last returning to 55th SRW as an RC-135W in August 1985. The RC-135W was essentially identical to the RC-135V, the main differences being the RC-135W's thrust-reversing TF33-P5 engines (the RC-135V's TF33-P9s lacked thrust reversers), slightly different in-flight refuelling receptacles and, initially, different designs of 'cheek' sensor fairings; RC-135Vs featured shorter (Martin) cheeks, while RC-135W featured longer (E-Systems) cheeks that encroached on the crew entry doors. TDY deployments to Europe were to RAF Mildenhall, UK (with 306th SW; from 1989 2d SS, 306th SW), and Hellenikon AB, Greece (with 922d SS, 306th SW). European Rivet Joint PARPRO operations focussed upon military and naval facilities within the Murmansk and Archangelsk Oblasts in the north-western USSR; Soviet/WarPac facilities adjacent to the Baltic Sea, along the Iron Curtain (known as 'The Fence') between West Germany and East Germany/Czechoslovakia; and 'over the top' flights between Mildenhall and Eielson. Hellenikon operations covered the eastern Mediterranean, Middle East and North Africa. Far East operations (TDY with 376th SW from Kadena) included peripheral flights off the Soviet, Chinese and North Korean coasts.

The RC-135U Combat Sent conducted specialised ELINT, focussing on hostile radars and other emitters. Example missions from 1980 include RC-135Us collecting signals from the 5N62 ('Square Pair') fire control radar of the Soviet S-200 (SA-5 'Gammon') SAM system and the Swiss Super Fledermaus fire control radar. A notable sortie occurred on 3 June 1985. Forward deployed to Souda Bay, Crete, while on TDY with 306th SW, the RC-135U was flying an ELINT mission against the Soviet aircraft carrier *Kiev*, in the Black Sea. When the *Kiev* understandably switched off its radars, weapons systems and communications, pilot Major John 'Box' Elder mischievously lined the RC-135U up as though on final approach to the Soviet carrier, with gear and flaps extended. With the ultra-low RC-135U rapidly approaching, the concerned Soviet crew switched their radars back on and even attempted to make radio contact in English. Therefore, the RC-135U successfully collected the desired signals. The Soviets immediately lodged a formal complaint through the US State Department. When the RC-135U's crew later returned to the US, following the deployment's conclusion, General Bennie L. Davies, CINCSAC, met them to officially admonish them never to repeat anything like that again, while also giving them unofficial congratulations. RC-135Us occasionally co-operated with SR-71s; the high and fast SR-71 causing Soviet air defences to come alive, the RC-135U then collecting the resulting signals. Three RC-135Us were originally converted from RC-135Cs, two (64-14847/64-14849) funded by the USAF, one (63-9792) by the Central Intelligence Agency (CIA). When the CIA withdrew funding for the third RC-135U (believing satellites could achieve similar results), it was modified into the eighth RC-135V (conversion completed by 1977), leaving two RC-135Us with 55th SRW.

Above: RC-135W 62-4134 of the 55th SRW. This was the fourth RC-135M to become an RC-135W, modified in 1981. (NARA)

Right: An overhead view of RC-135W 62-4134. (NARA)

Major Richard Davis, left, and Captain Chris Hofstad of the 38th SRS fly a 55th SRW RC-135 over Texas during a training mission. (NARA)

Staff Sergeants Heidi Carter and Mark Stephen, of 6949th Electronic Security Squadron, monitor equipment in a 55th SRW RC-135. As well as 38th SRS cockpit crews and 343d SRS electronic warfare officers (known as Ravens) and in-flight maintenance technicians, the 6949th ESS made up the final portion of the RC-135 crew. The 6949th ESS, which was assigned to Electronic Security Command rather than SAC, provided on-board intelligence specialists. (NARA)

RC-135V 64-14844 of the 55th SRW taxiing at Mildenhall in 1988 while on TDY with the 306th SW. This had been the fourth RC-135C converted into an RC-135V, modified during 1974/5. Notable are the shorter and deeper Martin cheeks of the RC-135V, compared to the E-Systems cheeks on RC-135Ws at this time. (Mike Freer – Touchdown Aviation, via Wikimedia Commons)

RC-135W 62-4135 taxiing at Mildenhall in 1981 while on TDY with the 306th SW. This had been the first RC-135M converted to RC-135W standard, modified during 1978-80. It shows off the longer and less deep E-Systems cheeks of the RC-135W. In the 1990s RC-135Vs, and RC-135Us, also adopted the longer E-Systems cheeks in place of their Martin cheeks. (Mike Freer – Touchdown Aviation, via Wikimedia Commons)

Above: RC-135U 64-14847 at Mildenhall. This had been the first RC-135C converted into an RC-135U. Here it sports non-standard and unofficial shark's mouth markings. (Mike Freer – Touchdown Aviation, via Wikimedia Commons)

Right: Another view of RC-135U 64-14847 landing at Mildenhall; it lacks the shark's mouth at the time of this 1988 image. (Mike Freer – Touchdown Aviation, via Wikimedia Commons)

The 55th SRW EC/RC-135 cockpit crews had use of a number of trainers. J57-turbojet-powered KC-135A (ARR) 61-0293 served as a 55th SRW trainer. The unofficial 'ARR' designation denoted rare 'Air Refuelling Receiver' KC-135s featuring in-flight-refuelling receptacles. In 1985 61-0293 became the prototype KC-135R, subsequently reassigned elsewhere. TF33-turbofan-powered KC-135E (ARR) 59-1514 became the primary turbofan EC/RC-135 trainer from 31 August 1982. This KC-135E (ARR) was due to be replaced by 6th SW's RC-135T. As noted previously, however, this crashed in 1985 before it could be transferred to 55th SRW. Therefore, the KC-135E (ARR) was retained until a replacement could be found, and was even retained by 55th SRW after the dedicated trainer arrived. The dedicated trainer was TC-135W 62-4129, converted from a C-135B and delivered to 55th SRW on 22 April 1988. The various trainers were also utilised for support duties, including ferrying 55th SRW personnel to overseas locations.

KC-135E (ARR) 59-1514, used as a TF33-powered trainer by 55th SRW. This had been the first KC-135E conversion, and is seen here in 1982 immediately after modification. It is in overall FS 17178 silver/ aluminium. (NARA)

A notable mission involving the TC-135W occurred in 1989. The Prevention of Dangerous Military Activities accord was signed between the USA and the USSR on 12 June 1989, establishing procedures to prevent the use of force in response to accidental military contacts, incidents and accidents. This included preventing accidental attacks on each other's aircraft should one stray into the opponent's airspace.

December 1989 saw related joint US-Soviet flights over the Mediterranean Sea and Bering Strait. One flight saw a Soviet Tu-95 'Bear' and the 55th SRW TC-135W rendezvous over the Bering Sea. The two aircraft separated, proceeding into the Air Defence Identification Zone (ADIZ) of the other nation (but not entering the opposing nation's airspace), to be intercepted by USAF F-15s and PVO Su-27s respectively. The 'Bear' and TC-135W crews spoke to the pilots of the opposing interceptors, and ground/sea-based controllers, testing the accord's procedures. The accord came into full effect on 1 January 1990. The wing also operated C-135A/E Command Support Aircraft (CSA), primarily supporting co-located Headquarters SAC, including transporting senior SAC personnel overseas. Another duty was flying Operational Readiness Inspection (ORI) teams to various SAC bases on unannounced visits. At any moment, an ORI team might land without notice at a SAC base and require the wing commander to execute his war plan. If the wing failed, the commander could lose his job. At the start of the 1980s two CSA C-135As were operated. C-135A 60-0376 had its J57s replaced by TF33-PW-102s in April 1982, becoming a C-135E, but was transferred out of 55th SRW in June 1983; the other C-135A (60-0378, featuring a VIP interior) remained with the wing for the rest of the decade (lack of funds precluding it receiving TF33s). On 13 September 1983, former testbed NKC-135A 55-3119 transferred from Air Force Systems Command (AFSC) to 55th SRW to act as a CSA. Later plans to re-engine it to NKC-135E with TF33-PW-102s were shelved. Finally, 55th SRW also operated KC-135A 57-2589 with call sign 'CASEY 01' as CINCSAC's personal VIP transport, becoming a TF33-PW-102-powered KC-135E in 1983, retaining its CINCSAC role. One notable non-flying 55th SRW unit was 55th Mobile Command and Control Squadron (MCCS), a survivable, road-mobile, truck-based, backup command post, ready to leave Offutt AFB at a moment's notice. They could set up an independent, survivable command centre far away from likely nuclear attacks. The 55th SRW won the 1984 P. T. Cullen Award. The 55th SRW was assigned to 4th AD, reassigned to 57th AD on 1 April 1980, 12th AD on 1 October 1982 and finally to 14th AD on 1 October 1985; all these ADs were under 15th AF.

The 68th BMW at Seymour Johnson AFB, North Carolina, was assigned 51st BMS with B-52Gs and 911th AREFS with KC-135As. The 68th BMW inactivated on 30 September 1982 as did 51st BMS (allowing 46th BMS/319th BMW at Grand Forks AFB to replace its B-52Hs with B-52Gs). On the same day 68th Air Refueling Group, Heavy (AREFG) activated at Seymour Johnson, controlling 911th AREFS, the latter converting to KC-10As from 1985. On 5 March 1986 two 911th AREFS KC-10As (*Gold 11* and *Gold 21*, temporarily operating out of Pease AFB, while Seymour Johnson was undergoing runway repairs) were 'dragging' nine Marine A-4s from MCAS Cherry Point to Bodø, Norway, with a stopover at Lajes Field, Azores. Deteriorating weather at Lajes forced a diversion to the Portuguese island of Santa Maria, itself suffering deteriorating weather. *Gold 11* and its group of A-4s landed, followed by another group of three A-4s (escorted by a Marine KC-130 that had launched from Lajes to assist); however, the third of these A-4s crashed on landing, scattering debris over the end of the runway, closing it to further landings. *Gold 21* and its three remaining A-4s were running out of fuel and preparing to ditch. *Gold 11* quickly refuelled and took off again, getting airborne in time to avoid the debris-strewn end of the fogged-in runway. *Gold 11* rendezvoused with, and refuelled, *Gold 21* and its three A-4s, allowing them all to proceed safely to NAS Rota, Spain. Captain Marc D. Felman and the remainder of *Gold 11*'s crew received the 1986 Mackay Trophy for their heroic actions. On 1 October 1986 68th AREFG became 68th AREFW and 344th AREFS was added. The 344th/911th AREFS subsequently shared the wing's KC-10As (eighteen by 1989). KC-135As had red/blue checkerboard tail markings; the KC-10As adopted 'Wright Flyer' markings. The 68th BMW/AREFG/AREFW was assigned to 42d AD (under 8th AF), later assigned directly to 8th AF on 16 June 1988.

A 68th AREFW KC-10A refuels TAC F-15Cs of the 94th TFS, 1st TFW, during exercise Coronet Warrior in 1987. Coronet Warrior was a TAC spares logistics exercise, with the F-15 unit isolated at its home station with a representative spares package. It then conducted wartime sortie rates for thirty days to explore how many aircraft would remain fully mission capable (FMC) at the end of the period. Predictions of just four remaining FMC were considerably exceeded, as seventeen remained FMC. (NARA)

The 90th SMW at Francis E. Warren AFB, Wyoming, was assigned 319th, 320th, 321st and 400th SMS (with silos respectively north-east, east, south-east and north of Francis E. Warren). Each was equipped with fifty LGM-30Gs, until 400th SMS began to receive fifty replacement LGM-118A Peacekeepers. Personnel training and facility preparation began in June 1985. The first Peacekeepers went on alert on 10 October 1986. On 22 December 1986 400th SMS achieved IOC, placing the first flight of ten Peacekeepers on alert. Full operational capability occurred in December 1988, when all fifty Peacekeepers became operational. The wing won the 1983 Omaha Trophy and the 1984 Blanchard Trophy. The 90th SMW was assigned to 4th AD (under 15th AF), later assigned directly to 15th AF on 23 August 1988.

The 91st SMW at Minot AFB was assigned 740th, 741st and 742d SMS (with silos respectively south, south-west and north-west of Minot), each with fifty LGM-30Gs. The wing won the Blanchard Trophy in 1988; it was assigned to 57th AD (under 15th AF).

A 92d BMW B-52G being loaded with ALCMs at Fairchild AFB in 1984. A specially designed remote control hydraulic trailer is used to attach the pylon, which is already carrying its six ALCMs. (NARA)

Slightly further down the Fairchild flight line than the last image, also during 1984, are 92d BMW B-52Gs, along with KC-135As in the distance. The nearest B-52G is 57-6479, which was the first 92d BMW B-52G to be repainted in the new 'Strategic Camouflage Scheme'. It can be readily compared to the previous SIOP scheme on the B-52Gs behind. (NARA)

An aerial view of 92d BMW B-52G 57-6479 showing off its new Strategic Camouflage Scheme on 30 July 1984. On 16 October 1984 57-6479 departed Fairchild for a scheduled night training mission. While flying in and out of snow showers, the B-52G's right wing struck the north crest of Hunts Mesa in Monument Valley. The aircraft continued to travel for another 3,465 feet before crashing onto a lower southern bluff of Hunts Mesa. Five of the seven on board ejected successfully; tragically, Sergeant David W. Felix (gunner) was killed as his parachute failed to deploy, while Colonel William L Ivy (92d BMW deputy commander for operations, on board as an observer) was also killed as he was in the observer's jump seat without ejection capability. (NARA)

B-52H 60-0061 (with nose art and named *ABOUT AVERAGE*) of the 92d BMW is prepared for take-off during exercise Giant Warrior '89, while deployed to Osan AB, South Korea. Note that in the late 1980s wing shield emblems were added to the left-hand side of aircraft; hitherto they had been on the right-hand side. (NARA)

The 92d BMW at Fairchild AFB, Washington, was assigned 325th BMS with B-52Gs (ALCM-equipped from the early 1980s), converting to B-52Hs between 10 September 1985 and 28 May 1986. Also assigned were 43d and 92d AREFS, sharing KC-135As. The 43d AREFS won the 1986 Spaatz Trophy. The 92d BMW won the 1986 Fairchild Trophy. The wing's KC-135As adopted tail markings with 'Fairchild' titles and crowns on a royal blue stripe. By 1989 the wing operated around eighteen B-52Hs and twenty-three KC-135As. The 92d BMW was assigned to 47th AD (under 15th AF), reassigned to 57th AD (15th AF) on 23 January 1987 and reassigned directly to 15th AF on 15 June 1988.

The 93d BMW at Castle AFB, California, was assigned 328th BMS with B-52G/Hs (operating only B-52Gs from 19 September 1983). This aircrew training unit had a secondary operational mission. Due to high training utilisation (including endless landing patterns), aircraft were regularly rotated through the wing to prevent excessive airframe hours being accrued. Also assigned were 93d and 924th AREFS. The 93d AREFS had been the USAF's first KC-135 squadron, and conducted KC-135A aircrew training. It retained an EWO commitment along with its training mission, but did not stand alert. After academic training, each crew (pilot, co-pilot, navigator, and boom operator) received forty-five days of flight training with 93d AREFS; the unit trained thousands of KC-135 aircrew. The squadron also provided specialised shorter duration training to senior officers (such as wing commanders). For a period 93d AREFS sent instructor teams to ANG/AFRES units converting to KC-135s, helping develop in-house training programmes. Occasionally 93d AREFS crews deployed to meet its own EWO commitments or to meet needs exceeding the capability of 924th AREFS. The 93d AREFS added KC-135Rs from 1987. Meanwhile, 924th AREFS remained an operational KC-135A unit; although 93d BMW operated a mixed KC-135A/R fleet from 1987, 924th AREFS exclusively flew KC-135As. The 924th had the distinction of having SAC's first all-female crew on 10 June 1982, nicknamed 'Fair Force One'. Commanded by Captain Kelly S. C. Hamilton, then SAC's only female aircraft commander, they performed a 5-hour training mission, including refuelling a B-52. They were supported by two female mission schedulers from 93d BMW's training operations branch and an all-female ground crew. The five female flight crew members were not a permanent crew, although the three ground crew had been Castle's first permanent all-female ground crew. The 4017th CCTS provided KC-135/B-52G academic training; on 1 July 1986 329th CCTS activated, replacing 4017th CCTS and taking over its duties. The 330th Combat Flight Instructor Squadron (CFIS) activated on 24 August 1988; it taught the B-52 and KC-135 Combat Flight Instructors Courses. The wing adopted grey rook chess piece tail markings for its KC-135s and B-52Gs (with a black band on the KC-135s) during the decade. By 1989 the wing operated thirty-five B-52Gs and forty-five/nineteen KC-135A/Rs. The 93d BMW was assigned to 14th AD (under 15th AF), reassigned to 12th AD (15th AF) on 1 October 1985 and directly assigned to 15th AF from 15 July 1988.

The 96th BMW at Dyess AFB, Texas, was assigned 337th BMS with B-52Ds, converting to B-52Hs between 3 May and 4 November 1982. The last B-52H departed on 19 January 1985 and replacement B-1Bs were received from 29 June 1985. The 4018th CCTS was activated and assigned on 15 March 1985 as the B-1B training unit. This was replaced by 338th Strategic Bombardment Training Squadron (SBTS), which activated on 1 July 1986 (redesignated 338th CCTS on 1 January 1987). On 1 October 1986 96th BMW hosted SAC's first B-1B alert line. Also assigned was 917th AREFS with KC-135As; KC-135Rs were received at decade's end. On 4 October 1989 a 96th BMW crew diverted to Edwards AFB, making the first-ever nose-gear-up B-1B emergency landing. There was only minimal damage and no injuries; for this Captain Jeffrey K. Beene and his crew received the 1989 Mackay Trophy. The wing adopted markings featuring a longhorn cow skull superimposed over the Texas flag (toned-down on the B-1Bs, full-colour on the KC-135As). By 1989 96th BMW

B-52G 57-6483 of the resident 93d BMW seen on approach while flying training landing patterns at Castle AFB on 14 November 1989. This B-52G is in the overall FS 36081 dark grey 'Monochromatic Camouflage Scheme' that SAC introduced from 1988. In 1990 this was changed to overall FS 36118 medium grey. By the end of the 1980s B-52G/Hs could be found in the SIOP Scheme (with or without the repainted dark grey nose), the Strategic Camouflage Scheme and the Monochromatic Camouflage Scheme. (Mike Freer – Touchdown Aviation, via Wikimedia Commons)

Right: A 96th BMW B-1B during exercise Distant Mariner in 1988, during which it operated from Andersen AFB, Guam. (NARA)

Below: A KC-135A refuels a B-1B; both are 96th BMW aircraft. (NARA)

operated thirty-one B-1Bs and thirteen/two KC-135A/Rs. The wing was assigned to 12th AD (under 15th AF) until being assigned directly to 15th AF on 15 July 1988.

The 97th BMW at Blytheville AFB, Arkansas (renamed Eaker AFB in 1988), was assigned 340th BMS with B-52Gs (later with ALCMs) and 97th AREFS with KC-135As. On 21 January 1985, Lieutenant Colonel David E. Faught, a 97th BMW evaluator pilot, saved his eight crew members and prevented the loss of his KC-135A, which was unable to lower its nose gear when preparing to land after a 6-hour sortie. With weather deteriorating and fuel low, the KC-135A reverse-refuelled from an EC-135. Centre-of-gravity restrictions limited fuel onload to 8,000 lb (3630 kg) at a time, requiring hook-ups every 20 minutes. A KC-10 relieved the EC-135, but this soon ran low on fuel. The Blytheville strip-alert KC-135A launched to refuel the KC-10, which continued to reverse-refuel the stricken KC-135A. After nearly 13 hours airborne, with darkness approaching and still unable to lower the nose gear Lieutenant Colonel Faught decided to make a nose-gear-up landing at Blytheville, which was achieved with minimal damage. Lieutenant Colonel Faught received the 1985 Mackay Trophy. The wing adopted red/white checkerboard KC-135A tail markings, later replacing those with a flaming spear on a blue band; at the same time the B-52Gs adopted toned down flaming spear markings. The 97th BMW won the 1985 Fairchild Trophy and the 1988 Omaha Trophy. The wing's mission expanded to include conventional bombing, sea search/surveillance, and aerial mining in 1987. By 1989 the wing operated eight B-52Gs and eleven KC-135As. The wing was assigned to 42d AD (under 8th AF) until being assigned directly to 8th AF on 16 June 1988.

The 99th Strategic Weapons Wing (SWW) at Ellsworth AFB activated on 10 August 1989. The non-flying unit conducted advanced strategic bombing and electronic warfare tactics training for bomber crews utilising the Strategic Training Route Complex (STRC), a series of fourteen training routes for bomber low-level flight training. STRC, developed from 1978 and opened on 1 July 1981, included mobile radar bombing sites in Wyoming and Idaho, and simulated strategic penetration of the northern USSR. As the routes were in the western USA, this disadvantaged eastern-based units, which had to expend flight hours to access the routes. The 25th Strategic Training Squadron (STS) activated on 1 July 1988, assigned directly to SAC; it was reassigned to 99th SWW on 10 August 1989 when the latter activated. The 25th STS provided STRC range control from its Strategic Weapons Center facility. The 99th SWW was assigned to 12th AD (under 8th AF).

The 100th AREFW at Beale AFB was assigned 9th and 349th AREFS with KC-135Qs, supporting the co-located 9th SRW SR-71s. The 9th AREFS inactivated on 27 January 1982 (reactivating on 1 October 1982, reassigned to 22d AREFW at March AFB). The former 9th AREFS personnel were used to form 350th AREFS, which activated at Beale on 28 January 1982. On 15 March 1983 100th AREFW was inactivated; 349th and 350th AREFS were transferred to 9th SRW (q.v.). The 100th AREFW had been assigned to 14th AD (under 15th AF).

The 301st AREFW at MALMSTROM AFB, Montana, activated on 5 January 1988, only assigned KC-135R-equipped 91st AREFS, which activated the same day. Markings consisted of a bison skull superimposed over mountains and 'Malmstrom' titles. The wing was assigned directly to 15th AF, until being reassigned to the newly reactivated 40th AD (15th AF) on 7 July 1989.

The 305th AREFW at Grissom AFB, Indiana, was assigned 70th and 305th AREFS, operating pooled KC-135As, including KC-135A (ARR)s and KC-135Ds. (The four

A 100th AREFW KC-135Q refuels a 9th SRW SR-71A during 1981. The 100th SRW inactivated before SAC wings generally adopted wing markings, therefore never adopted such markings. (NARA)

KC-135Ds were unique, being former RC-135As modified to approximate KC-135A standard.) The KC-135As were upgraded into KC-135Rs during 1987–88. The 305th AREFS won the 1981 Spaatz Trophy. As well as the KC-135s, 70th AREFS also operated EC-135G/Ls for radio relay duties as part of PACCS. Five EC-135Ls were operated for much of the 1980s, although one had been transferred to 4th ACCS at Ellsworth by 1989. A single EC-135G was also operated for most of the decade as a radio relay aircraft. The other three EC-135Gs with 4th ACCS were operated in the ALCS role; the 70th AREFS EC-135G was nicknamed 'Miss Piggy' due to the increased weight of the added radio relay equipment. During 1987 70th AREFS swapped the EC-135G it operated with one of the other three 4th ACCS EC-135Gs. Two 70th AREFS EC-135Ls (*Radio Relay No. 1* and *Radio Relay No. 2*) were maintained on 15-minute ground alert at Grissom. The wing adopted black/white checkerboard tail markings for its KC/EC-135s during the decade. By 1989 305th AREFW operated three KC-135As, seven KC-135A (ARR)s, four KC-135Ds, twenty-three KC-135Rs and one KC-135R (ARR), as well as four EC-135Ls and an EC-135G. The 305th AREFW was assigned to 40th AD (under 8th AF), reassigned to 42d AD (8th AF) on 1 December 1982, and finally assigned directly to 8th AF on 16 June 1988.

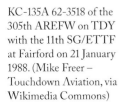

KC-135A 62-3518 of the 305th AREFW on TDY with the 11th SG/ETTF at Fairford on 21 January 1988. (Mike Freer – Touchdown Aviation, via Wikimedia Commons)

The 306th SW at RAF Mildenhall, England, controlled Mildenhall TDY tanker/ RC-135 deployments. Typically, there were around sixteen TDY tankers (including ANG/AFRES KC-135s) at Mildenhall. There would also usually be two or three RC-135s in Europe at any one time at Mildenhall, Hellenikon and elsewhere. Also assigned to 306th SW was 34th SS (TDY KC-135s, replaced by KC-10s from 1985) at Zaragoza AB, Spain, and 922d SS at Hellenikon AB, Greece (TDY KC-/RC-135s). The 922d SS won the 1981 P. T. Cullen Award, while 306th SW won the 1982 P. T. Cullen Award. The 306th SW's tankers, along with those of 11th SG, formed the ETTF. In the early 1980s Det 1, 306th SW activated to take over the KC-135 detachment at Keflavik, Iceland, formerly under 11th SG. On 1 October 1986 34th SS at Zaragoza was reassigned to 11th SG. On 1 January 1989 2d SS (formerly 2d BMS, inactivated at March AFB on 1 October 1982) activated at Mildenhall. This took control of the TDY tankers/RC-135s at Mildenhall, previously directly controlled by 306th SW. At Mildenhall TDY KC-135As were most common, although throughout the 1980s ANG/ AFRES KC-135Es and SAC KC-135Rs started to deploy. KC-135Qs would also be assigned, supporting Det 4, 9th SRW SR-71 operations, while occasionally KC-10As were deployed, notably for Operation El Dorado Canyon in 1986. Operations staff, maintenance personnel and some instructor pilots were permanently assigned, but aircraft, aircrews and crew chiefs were assigned to ETTF on a TDY basis. TDYs typically lasted up to forty-five days. UK-based KC-135s also often supported RAF QRA air defence aircraft (requiring fitment of flying boom drogue adaptors) and NATO E-3 Sentry AWACS aircraft. The 306th SW was assigned to 7th AD (itself directly assigned to SAC, until its reassignment to 8th AF on 31 Jan 1982).

The 308th SMW at Little Rock AFB, Arkansas, was assigned 373d and 374th SMS (with silos respectively north-east and north-west of Little Rock) with Titan IIs. Titan II wings consisted of two squadrons, each with just nine ICBMs (unlike Minuteman/ Peacekeeper wings with three or four squadrons, each with fifty missiles). Individual Titan II Launch Complexes (LCs) were numbered for their squadron, followed by an individual sequential number, i.e. 373-1 to 373-9 and 374-1 to 374-9. A major mishap occurred at LC 374–7, near Damascus, Arkansas, in 1980. Two Propellant Transfer System (PTS) airmen were checking the pressure on the oxidizer tank of the silo's Titan II at around 1830 hrs on 18 September. Using a ratchet, rather than the recently mandated torque wrench, the 8-lb (3.6-kg) socket for the oxidizer tank fell off the ratchet, dropping approximately 80 feet (24 m) before bouncing off a thrust mount and piercing the missile's skin over the first-stage fuel tank, causing it to leak a cloud of Aerozine 50 fuel. Aerozine 50 is hypergolic with the missile's oxidizer, nitrogen tetroxide, meaning that they spontaneously ignite on contact with each other. The crew evacuated the LC while additional teams arrived to tackle the hazardous situation. At around 0300 hrs on 19 September, just as another PTS team (Senior Airman David Lee Livingston and Sergeant Jeff K. Kennedy) were entering the LC to turn on an exhaust fan, the hypergolic fuel exploded, blowing the 740-ton silo door off and ejecting the Titan II's second stage and warhead. The second stage exploded clear of the silo; the W53 warhead landed around 100 feet (30 m) from the LC's entry gate. Fortunately, the warhead's safety features prevented nuclear detonation. Senior Airman Livingston received fatal injuries; twenty-one nearby personnel were injured. After daybreak the warhead was recovered and later sent to the Pantex weapons assembly plant, near Amarillo, Texas. LC 374–7 was not rebuilt after the mishap, with 374th SMS reduced to eight Titan IIs thereafter. The 308th SMW won the 1982 Omaha Trophy and the

1985 Blanchard Trophy. The 308th SMW became the last of the three Titan II wings to inactivate. The 374th SMS inactivated on 15 August 1986. The 373d SMS's LCs stood down between 20 June 1985, when 373-6 inactivated, and 4 May 1987, when the very last Titan II site (373–2) inactivated. The 373d SMS, along with 308th SMW itself, inactivated on 18 August 1987. The 308th SMW was assigned to 42d AD (under 8th AF), then reassigned to 19th AD (8th AF) on 1 December 1982 until inactivation.

The 319th BMW at Grand Forks AFB, North Dakota, was assigned 46th BMS (B-52Hs) and 905th AREFS (KC-135As). The 46th BMS, while retaining its strategic nuclear mission, was assigned to the Strategic Projection Force until 1982; it converted to former 68th BMW/Seymour Johnson B-52Gs between 3 May 1982 and 7 April 1983, then to B-1Bs during 1987–88. The 905th AREFS converted to KC-135Rs in 1986–87. In the late 1980s the wing adopted orange/blue bands and Grand Forks 'sunflake' markings for its B-1Bs and KC-135s. By 1989 the wing operated fifteen B-1Bs and eighteen KC-135Rs. The 319th BMW was assigned to 57th AD (under 15th AF), reassigned to 4th AD (15th AF) on 1 May 1982, reverting to 57th AD on 23 January 1987 and reassigned to 42d AD (under 8th AF) on 16 June 1988.

KC-135A 59-1475 of the 319th BMW while on TDY with the 306th SW/ETTF at Mildenhall on 8 March 1986. (Mike Freer – Touchdown Aviation, via Wikimedia Commons)

A 46th BMS crew runs towards their 319th BMW B-52H during a practice scramble alert at Grand Forks AFB in 1981. If the Cold War had ever turned hot, SAC crews would have had 15 minutes' warning to get their aircraft airborne before Soviet ICBMs/SLBMs destroyed their bases. (NARA)

Left: B-52H 61-0021 of the 319th BMW being readied for a mission at Grand Forks AFB during 1981. (NARA)

Below: B-1B 86-0114 of the 319th BMW visiting RAF Mildenhall in 1990. (Mike Freer – Touchdown Aviation, via Wikimedia Commons)

The 320th BMW at Mather AFB, California, was assigned 441st BMS with B-52Gs (nineteen assigned by 1989), adopting a conventional mission; they were the lead unit conducting Harpoon firing trials in 1983. The KC-135A-equipped 904th AREFS was also assigned, until it inactivated on 1 October 1986; this uniquely left 320th BMW without a tanker unit. However, the AFRES 314th AREFS, 940th AREFG (which converted from KC-135As to KC-135Es in 1986) shared the Mather ramp and supported 320th BMW alongside its other duties. The 441st BMS and 320th BMW inactivated on 30 September 1989, the last B-52G departing on 31 July, starting the gradual drawdown of the USAF B-52G fleet. Wing markings were a bear emblem for B-52Gs and a black/white checkerboard fin band with a superimposed yellow California map with brown bear for its KC-135As. The 320th BMW won the 1980 Fairchild Trophy. The 320th BMW was assigned to 14th AD, under 15th AF.

The 321st SMW at Grand Forks AFB was assigned 446th, 447th and 448th SMS (silos respectively north-west, west and south-west of Grand Forks); each had fifty LGM-30Gs. The wing won the 1987 Blanchard Trophy. The 321st SMW was assigned to 57th AD

Above left: KC-135A 57-1499 of the 320th BMW on TDY with the 306th SW/ETTF at Mildenhall on 22 September 1985. (Mike Freer – Touchdown Aviation, via Wikimedia Commons)

Above right: B-52G 57-6468, named *Eldership*, of the 320th BMW deployed to Andersen AFB, Guam for exercise Giant Warrior '89. The first B-52G produced, 57-6468 was retired in July 1989, shortly after it was photographed here. (NARA)

(under 15th AF), reassigned to 4th AD (15th AF) on 1 May 1982, reverting to 57th AD on 23 January 1987 and reassigned to 42d AD (under 8th AF) on 16 June 1988.

The 340th AREFG at Altus AFB, Oklahoma, was assigned KC-135A-equipped 11th AREFS. On 1 October 1984 340th AREFG was redesignated 340th AREFW, and a second squadron, 306th AREFS, was added. The wing converted to KC-135Rs during 1987; around the same time the wing replaced its light blue and silver diamonds tail markings with a blue Oklahoma map with superimposed Conestoga wagon. By 1989 the wing operated eighteen KC-135Rs. The 340th AREFG/AREFW was assigned to 19th AD (under 8th AF), until being reassigned directly to 15th AF on 16 June 1988.

The 341st SMW at Malmstrom AFB was assigned 10th, 12th, 490th and 564th SMS (silos respectively south-west, west, south-east and north-west of Malmstrom), each with fifty LGM-30Fs. The wing won the 1986 Blanchard Trophy. The 341st SMW was assigned to 47th AD (under 15th AF), reassigned to 4th AD (15th AF) on 23 January 1987, reassigned directly to 15th AF on 23 August 1988 and reassigned to 40th AD (15th AF) on 7 July 1989.

The 351st SMW at Whiteman AFB, Missouri, controlled 508th, 509th and 510th SMS (silos respectively north and east, south and south-west, and surrounding and to the west of Whiteman). Each squadron had fifty LGM-30Fs; however, ten 510th SMS missiles were equipped with the Emergency Rocket Communications System (ERCS), comprising two powerful UHF transmitters in place of their warheads. ERCS ensured control of US strategic forces after a Soviet attack, allowing national and military leaders to send pre-recorded attack orders to SAC bombers and missiles if land-based and airborne command and control systems were destroyed. ERCS-equipped LGM-30Fs would have been launched at a very high trajectory, transmitting nuclear 'go code' orders to receivers within its line of sight (bombers in flight and ground-based nuclear forces in the US and around the world) for up to 30 minutes. Used since the 1960s, ERCS was made redundant by the introduction of secure communications satellites, leading to withdrawal in 1991. The wing won the 1981 and 1989 Blanchard Trophies. The 351st SMW was assigned to 40th AD (under 8th AF), reassigned to 19th AD (8th AF) on 1 December 1982, then assigned directly to 8th AF on 13 June 1988.

The 376th SW at Kadena AB, Okinawa, Japan, was assigned 909th AREFS with KC-135A/Qs (with 'KADENA' markings). The 909th AREFS won the 1988 Spaatz Trophy. The 376th SW also supported TDY RC-135s deployed to Kadena. The 376th SW was assigned to the 3d AD (which was assigned directly to SAC, until reassignment to 15th AF on 31 January 1982).

The 379th BMW at Wurtsmith AFB, Michigan, was assigned 524th BMS, which became the second B-52G unit to equip with ALCMs from 1982. Also assigned was 920th AREFS with KC-135As (plus at least one KC-135Q). By 1989 the wing operated fifteen B-52Gs and five/one KC-135A/Qs. The 379th BMW won the 1987 Fairchild Trophy. Wing B-52Gs wore 'Triangle-K' tail markings, while KC-135As featured yellow/red vertical tail stripes, replaced during 1986–87 by a 'Corvette Blue' stripe with '379 BMW' and an eagle in gold. The 379th BMW was assigned to 40th AD (under 8th AF) until 8 June 1988 when it was reassigned directly to SAC.

Above: KC-135A 58-0113 of the 376th SW refuels 80th TFS, 8th TFW, F-16As participating in exercise Cope Thunder 86-1 in the Philippines. (NARA)

Left: KC-135s of the 376th SW in revetments at Kadena AB in 1988. Nearest, in full 376th SW markings, is KC-135A 60-0363, behind is KC-135Q 60-0344. (NARA)

Above: KC-135A 61-0298 of the 379th BMW on TDY with the 306th SW/ETTF at Mildenhall, performing missed approaches on 31 March 1986. (Mike Freer – Touchdown Aviation, via Wikimedia Commons)

Right: KC-135A 60-0331 of the 379th BMW on TDY with the 11th SG/ETTF at Fairford on 16 May 1988. Note the later wing markings on this KC-135A compared to the previous image. (Mike Freer – Touchdown Aviation, via Wikimedia Commons)

The 380th Bombardment Wing, Medium (also abbreviated to BMW) at Plattsburgh AFB, New York, was assigned 528th Bombardment Squadron, Medium (BMS) (with blue fin stripe) and 529th BMS (red fin stripe), both operating FB-111As. For FB-111A training, the wing was also assigned 4007th CCTS, which used 528th/528th BMS aircraft. On 1 July 1986 this inactivated and was replaced by newly activated 530th SBTS, redesignated 530th CCTS on 1 July 1987, continuing to utilise 528th/529th BMS aircraft. Also assigned was 310th and 380th AREFS, operating KC-135A/Qs (with the first KC-135R received by decade's end). Wing markings for the KC-135s were initially green/white diagonal tail stripes. In the late 1980s the FB-111s and KC-135s adopted a red 'Big Apple' with '380 BMW' titles; on the KC-135s these markings were on a white band with 'Plattsburgh' titles. In 1984 the wing won the Omaha and Fairchild Trophies. By 1989 the wing operated thirty-six FB-111As (eight of which were maintained on 24-hour alert) plus sixteen/one/fifteen KC-135A/R/Qs. The 380th BMW was assigned to 45th AD (under 8th AF), then reassigned directly to 8th AF on 29 March 1989.

The 381st SMW at McConnell AFB, Kansas, was assigned 532d and 533d SMS (silos respectively west and east of McConnell) with Titan IIs. While 532d SMS had

Above: KC-135Q 59-1462 of the 380th BMW on TDY with the 306th SW/ETTF at Mildenhall on 27 April 1984. (Mike Freer – Touchdown Aviation, via Wikimedia Commons)

Left: Captain Robert E. Millay, a radar navigation instructor with the 528th BMS, checks his arrival time from the cockpit of his 380th BMW FB-111A at Mather AFB, CA, during exercise Proud Shield '87. (NARA)

the usual nine silos, 533d SMS only had eight silos due to an accident at LC 533-7 on 24 August 1978 (an oxidizer leak that killed two personnel and caused the temporary evacuation of local communities). The damage was determined to be unrepairable and the silo was permanently closed. Therefore 381st SMW subsequently operated seventeen Titan IIs. The 381st SMW won the 1980 and 1983 Blanchard Trophies. With the Titan II force drawdown, 533d SMS decommissioned its silos, starting with LC 533-8 on 2 July 1984, and inactivated on 1 November 1985; it transferred its only remaining silo, LC 533-9, to 532d SMS. The drawdown of 532d SMS had got underway with the decommissioning of LC 532-5 on 10 August 1984. By 1986 only five remained: LCs 532-4, 532-6, 532-8 and 532-9, plus 533-9, which had transferred from the 533d. The latter became the final LC to decommission, on 27 May 1986. Finally, on 8 August 1986 532d SMS and 381st SMW inactivated. The 381st SMW had been assigned to 19th AD (under 8th AF).

The 384th AREFW at McConnell AFB was assigned KC-135A-equipped 91st and 384th AREFS, becoming the first KC-135R recipient from 1984. On 1 July 1987 384th AREFW became 384th BMW; on the same day 91st AREFS inactivated (reactivated six months later and assigned to 301st AREFW), and 28th BMS activated, joining 384th AREFS in the wing, the latter operating sixteen KC-135Rs by 1989. The 28th BMS (previously a 19th BMW B-52G unit, until inactivation on 1 October 1983) became the sixth and final B-1B squadron (384th BMW becoming the fourth and final B-1B wing), finally receiving sixteen B-1Bs during 1988. The wing's KC-135s adopted light blue/insignia blue diamond checkerboard tail markings, replaced later in the decade by a variety of 'Keeper of the Plains' or 'McConnell' titles, sometimes retaining the blue diamond checkerboard. The B-1Bs adopted a blue stripe with 'Keeper of the Plains' titles and a Native American. The 384th AREFW was assigned to 19th AD (under 8th AF) until 1 July 1987 when it was assigned directly to SAC.

A 381st SMW Titan II re-entry vehicle is lowered by crane onto a trailer for transport from its silo back to McConnell AFB after deactivation. This was at LC 533-8, the first 381st SMW Launch Complex to be deactivated in July 1984. (NARA)

A 384th AREFW KC-135R on TDY with the ETTF refuels 50th TFW F-16Cs as they deploy from Hahn AB, West Germany, to Zaragoza AB, Spain, for exercise Sabre Thunder, a weapons training deployment during June 1987. The following month, the 384th AREFW became the 384th BMW when a B-1B squadron was added to the wing. (NARA)

The 390th SMW at Davis-Monthan AFB, Arizona, was assigned 570th and 571st SMS (silos respectively north and west, and south, of Davis-Monthan) each operating nine Titan IIs. The 390th SMW became the first of the three Titan II wings to inactivate. The 571st SMS decommissioned its first silo (LC 571-6) on 29 September 1982. When 571st SMS inactivated on 2 December 1983, its two remaining LCs (571-8 and 571-9) transferred to 570th SMS. The 570th SMS had started to decommission LCs prior to 571st SMS, when LC 570-9's Titan II was removed to be used for testing on 2 July 1982. The final 570th SMS Titan II silo (LC 570-5) was decommissioned on 21 May 1984; 570th SMS and 390th SMW inactivated on 31 July 1984. The 390th SMW was assigned to 12th AD (under 15th AF).

The 410th BMW at K. I. Sawyer AFB, Michigan, was assigned 644th BMS with B-52Hs. This gained ALCMs during the 1980s and had been the first unit to receive SRAM (in 1973) and the first to receive Electro-Optical Viewing System (EVS) equipped B-52s. It was also the first unit to receive AGM-129A Advanced Cruise

Propellant Transfer System technicians from the 390th Missile Maintenance Squadron offload liquid oxidizer from the Titan II at site LC 571-6, the first 390th SMW Titan II missile site to be formally deactivated in 1982. (NARA)

A 410th BMW B-52H viewed from a tanker in 1988. It shows off its SIOP camouflage, with the formerly white nose repainted, along with the cockpit area, in FS 36081 dark grey to make it less conspicuous. (NARA)

Missiles, although delivery of fully operational missiles was delayed until 1990. In March 1980, two 644th BMS B-52Hs made a nonstop, 42.5-hour, round-the-world flight; the crews received the 1980 Mackay Trophy. Also assigned was KC-135A-equipped 46th AREFS; on 30 September 1985 a second KC-135A unit – 307th AREFS – was activated and assigned. The 410th BMW won the 1980 Omaha Trophy and 46th AREFS won the 1982 Spaatz Trophy. The wing adopted red/white vertical tail stripe markings for its KC-135As, replaced in 1987–88 by a rainbow with 'KI SAWYER' titles; the B-52Hs also adopted a rainbow. By 1989 the wing operated approximately eighteen B-52Hs and twenty-two KC-135As. The 410th BMW was assigned to 40th AD (under 8th AF) until 8 January 1988 when it was reassigned directly to 8th AF.

The 416th BMW at Griffiss AFB, New York, was assigned the B-52G-equipped 668th BMS. It was the first unit to receive ALCMs, becoming operational with ALCMs from 16 December 1982. The unit also had a conventional role, demonstrating various surge efforts, simulating massed conventional attacks, and deploying to various austere 'bare base' airfields. The unit also tested the B-52 Digital Automatic Flight Control System. Also assigned was KC-135A-equipped 41st AREFS; the first KC-135R being received at decade's end. By 1989 the wing operated nine B-52Gs and thirteen/one KC-135A/Rs. During the decade the wing adopted blue/yellow vertical tail stripes for its KC-135s, replaced in 1987–88 by a Statue of Liberty and 'GRIFFISS' titles, the latter being adopted by the B-52Gs around the same time. The 416th BMW was assigned to 45th AD (under 8th AF), reassigned to 40th AD (8th AF) on 1 December 1982 and reassigned directly to 8th AF on 8 June 1988.

The 509th BMW at Pease AFB, New Hampshire, was assigned FB-111A-equipped 393d BMS and 715th BMS and KC-135A-equipped 509th AREFS. By 1989 the wing

An AGM-86B ALCM-toting 416th BMW B-52G, in the Strategic Camouflage Scheme, during 1988; fuel streams down its spine after refuelling. Notable here are the curved wing root leading edge 'strakelets' added to the ninety-eight (of 167 remaining) B-52Gs that received ALCM compatibility. This allowed Soviet satellites to identify ALCM-capable B-52Gs, in keeping with arms control treaty verification agreements. B-52Hs received no such visual modification when gaining ALCM compatibility, as all B-52Hs became ALCM compatible, and the H model was clearly identifiable due to its turbofans. (NARA)

A closer view of the ALCM-equipped 416th BMW B-52G seen in the previous image. (NARA)

A 416th BMW B-52G about to land at Elmendorf AFB, Alaska, while participating in air defence exercise Amalgam Warrior '88. (NARA)

operated twenty-five FB-111As (which adopted New Hampshire map silhouette markings) and thirteen KC-135As (which initially adopted red/blue diagonal tail stripes, later replaced with a red Pegasus on a white band). The 509th BMW won the 1981, 1982 and 1983 Fairchild Trophies. The wing was assigned to 45th AD (under 8th AF) until 29 March 1989 when reassigned directly to 8th AF.

The non-flying 544th Strategic Intelligence Wing (SIW) at Offutt AFB, assigned directly to SAC headquarters, was the command's unique in-house intelligence outfit. With a force of approximately 1,000 officer and enlisted personnel, it was the only US intelligence community organisation with the capability and charter to perform complete all-source intelligence fusion. Producing strategic intelligence essential to SAC's mission, it operated the USAF's largest photo-processing, imagery interpretation, ELINT processing and all-source analysis activities. A primary task was supporting indications and warning analysis relating to the threat of Soviet attack on North America. It included a unique Strategic Targeting Intelligence Center

A 509th BMW FB-111A in the SIOP scheme takes off from Pease AFB in 1984. (NARA)

A 509th BMW FB-111A displays some of its ordnance options in 1989. Underwing are twenty BDU-50 500-pound practice bombs (the training version of the Mk 82). In the front row are, from the left: an M-117D 750-pound high-drag bomb, twelve Mk 106 5-pound practice bombs, six BDU-50/Mk 82 500-pound high-drag training bombs, twelve more Mk 106 practice bombs and a CBU-89 cluster bomb. In the second row are, from the left: B83 and B61 nuclear bomb trainers, two SRAM trainers and one more each of the B61 and B83 nuclear bomb trainers. (NARA)

Two 509th BMW FB-111As prepare for take-off at Pease AFB. (NARA)

The FB-111As seen in the previous image during their training sortie. The lead FB-111A carries a load of twenty BDU-50/Mk 82 500-pound practice bombs. Their later Strategic Camouflage Scheme is effective against the terrain here. (NARA)

One of the 509th BMW FB-111As pickles its load of BDU-50/Mk 82 500-pound practice bombs over the target range. The bombs are fitted with BSU-49 air inflatable retard (AIR) fins, the 'ballute' retarders of which can be seen inflating to slow the bombs, essential in low-level release to prevent damage to the delivering aircraft when the bombs explode. (NARA)

A 509th BMW FB-111A, carrying 600-US gal fuel tanks, arrives at Minot AFB for participation in Proud Shield '88. FB-111As in the Strategic Camouflage Scheme were nicknamed 'Dark Varks'. (NARA)

KC-135As and an FB-111A of the 509th BMW on the Pease AFB flight line during Proud Shield '87. The nearest KC-135A features the earlier tail stripes, the others the later markings. (NARA)

Of all the missile and space system launches at Vandenberg, more than half were made by agencies other than SAC. Here NASA Space Shuttle Orbiter OV-101 *Enterprise* is on the launch tower at Vandenberg AFB's Space Launch Complex 6 (SLC-6) during 1985. *Enterprise* was the first orbiter constructed, but was intended for atmospheric test flights and was not capable of spaceflight. It was being used here for fit tests at Vandenberg's newly constructed Space Shuttle launch facilities, intended to serve as the Space Shuttle's west coast launch site. The extensive reconstruction work at SLC-6 cost over $4 billion. However, the USAF terminated the Space Shuttle programme at Vandenberg in 1989 and no Space Shuttles were ever launched from there. (NARA)

with trajectory, weaponeering, targeting and contingency support missions. The 544th SIW's intelligence also directly supported the JSTPS which maintained SIOP. It also maintained an enemy force structure database; during the 1980s this expanded to include not only identifying, but also tracking, 'strategic relocatable targets' to support adaptive retargeting. These strategic relocatable targets were the newly fielded Soviet mobile ICBMs – the rail-based variants of the RT-23 Molodets (SS-24 Scalpel) and the road-mobile RT-2PM Topol (SS-25 Sickle).

The 4392d Aerospace Support Group (ASG), redesignated 4392d Aerospace Support Wing (ASW) on 1 July 1987, was another non-flying unit and operated the base at Vandenberg AFB; it was assigned to 1st SAD, itself directly assigned to SAC.

Also at Vandenberg, and directly assigned to 1st SAD, was 4315th CCTS; this trained all USAF ICBM crews.

Air Divisions

Eighth Air Force (headquartered at Barksdale AFB) was responsible for SAC units in the eastern half of the USA, and Fifteenth Air Force (March AFB) for those in the western USA. Air Divisions were allocated to each, in turn controlling the majority of SAC's wings, although from 1987 to 1988 some wings were assigned directly to the Numbered Air Forces or to SAC itself. Some ADs were also directly allocated to SAC.

There was reorganisation during 1982. Overseas ADs were reassigned from SAC headquarters to the Numbered Air Forces; on 31 January 1982, 3d and 7th ADs were reassigned to 15th and 8th AF, respectively. The CONUS ADs were also realigned. The 8th AF realignment placed what would subsequently become the last two Titan II wings under a single commander to oversee Titan II's coming phase-out. Other changes within 8th and 15th AFs balanced division strengths and distances between division headquarters and subordinate units. There was further considerable reorganisation during 1987–89.

The 1st Strategic Aerospace Division (SAD) (Vandenberg AFB) was directly assigned to SAC until reassignment to 15th AF on 1 September 1988. 1st SAD was responsible for operational testing of missile systems, supporting missile launchings by SAC and other agencies, and training SAC missilemen. Directly assigned was 4315th CCTS and 4392d ASG/ASW.

The 3d AD (Andersen AFB, moving to Hickam AFB, Hawaii, on 12 September 1988), was directly assigned to SAC until reassignment to 15th AF on 31 January 1982. Controlling SAC operations in the Western Pacific, Far East, and South East Asia, components were Andersen's 43rd SW/BMW and Kadena's 376th SW.

The 4th AD (Francis E. Warren AFB) was assigned to 15th AF; components were Ellsworth's 28th BMW/44th SMW (both assigned until 1 May 1982 and again 23 January 1987–15 July 1988), Offutt's 55th SRW (until 1 April 1980), Francis E. Warren's 90th SMW and Malmstrom's 341st SMW (both assigned until 23 August 1988), and Grand Forks' 319th BMW/321st SMW (both assigned between 1 May 1982 and 23 January 1987). The 4th AD inactivated on 23 August 1988.

The 7th AD (Ramstein AB, West Germany) was directly assigned to SAC, until reassignment to 8th AF on 31 January 1982. Controlling SAC operations in Europe, components were Fairford's 11th SG, Mildenhall's 306th SW, and Alconbury's 17th RW (from 1 October 1982).

The 12th AD (Dyess AFB, moving to Ellsworth AFB on 15 July 1988) was assigned to 15th AF until reassignment to 8th AF on 1 July 1989. Components were March's 22d BMW/AREFW (until 1 October 1985), Davis-Monthan's 390th SMW (until inactivation on 31 July 1984), Dyess' 96th BMW (until 15 July 1988), Offutt's 55th SRW (1 October 1982–1 October 1985). Castle's 93d BMW (1 October 1985–15 July 1988). Ellsworth's 28th BMW/44th SMW (from 15 July 1988) and Ellsworth's 99th SWW (from 10 August 1989).

The 14th AD (Beale AFB) was assigned to 15th AF. Components were Beale's 9th SRW (throughout) and 100th AREFW (until its 15 March 1983 inactivation), Castle's 93d BMW (until 1 October 1985), Mather's 320th BMW (until 30 September 1989), Eielson's 6th SW/SRW (from 1 October 1985), Offutt's 55th SRW (from 1 October 1985) and March's 22d AREFW (23 January 1987–1 July 1988).

The 19th AD (Carswell AFB) was assigned to 8th AF. Components were Barksdale's 2d BMW (until 1 December 1982), McConnell's 381st SMW (until its 8 August 1986 inactivation) and 384th AREFW (until 1 July 1987), Carswell's 7th BMW (until 13 June 1988), Altus' 340th AREFG/AREFW (until 16 June 1988), Little Rock's 308th SMW (from 1 December 1982 until inactivation on 18 August 1987) and Whiteman's 351st SMW (1 December 1982–13 June 1988). The 19th AD inactivated on 30 September 1988.

The 40th AD (Wurtsmith AFB) was assigned to 8th AF. Components were Grissom's 305th AREFW (until 1 December 1982), Whiteman's 351st SMW (until 1 December 1982), Wurtsmith's 379th BMW (until 8 June 1988), K. I. Sawyer's 410th BMW (until 8 January 1988) and Griffiss' 416th BMW (1 December 1982–8 June 1988). The 40th AD inactivated on 8 June 1988. It reactivated on 7 July 1989, reassigned to 15th AF and relocated to Malmstrom AFB, where it took on host responsibilities for 301st AREFW and 341st SMW.

The 42d AD (Blytheville/Eaker AFB) was assigned to 8th AF. Components were Little Rock's 308th SMW (until 1 December 1982), Barksdale's 2d BMW and Grissom's 305th AREFW (1 December 1982–16 June 1988) and Robins' 19th BMW/AREFW, Blytheville/Eaker's 97th BMW and Seymour Johnson's 68th BMW/AREFG/AREFW (until 16 June 1988). On 16 June 1988 42d AD relocated to Grand Forks AFB, where 319th BMW and 321st SMW became its components.

The 45th AD (Pease AFB) was assigned to 8th AF. Components were Griffiss' 416th BMW (until 1 December 1982), Loring's 42d BMW, Plattsburgh's 380th BMW and Pease's 509th BMW (all until 29 March 1989). The 45th AD inactivated on 15 June 1989.

The 47th AD (Fairchild AFB) was assigned to 15th AF. Components were Eielson's 6th SW (until 1 October 1985), Mather's 320th BMW (1 October 1982–23 January 1987), March's 22d AREFW (1 October 1985–23 January 1987), Fairchild's 92d BMW (until 23 January 1987) and Malmstrom's 341st SMW (until 23 January 1987). The 47th AD inactivated on 27 February 1987.

The 57th AD (Minot AFB) was assigned to 15th AF. Components were Minot's 5th BMW/91st SMW (throughout), Offutt's 55th SRW (1 April 1980--1 October 1982), Grand Forks' 319th BMW/321st SMW (until 1 May 1982 and again 23 January 1987–16 June 1988), Ellsworth's 28th BMW/44th SMW (1 May 1982–23 January 1987) and Fairchild's 92d BMW (23 January 1987–15 June 1988).

Several wings were reassigned directly to the Numbered Air Forces or to SAC headquarters late in the decade.

Eighth Air Force was directly assigned K. I. Sawyer's 410th BMW (from 8 January 1988), Griffiss' 416th BMW (from 8 June 1988), Carswell's 7th BMW and Whiteman's 351st SMW (from 13 June 1988), Barksdale's 2d BMW, Eaker's 97th BMW, Robins' 19th AREFW, Seymour Johnson's 68th AREFW and Grissom's 305th AREFW (from 16 June 1988) and Loring's 42d BMW, Plattsburgh's 380th BMW and Pease's 509th BMW (from 29 March 1989).

Fifteenth Air Force was directly assigned Malmstrom's 301st AREFW (8 January 1988–7 July 1989) and 341st SMW (23 August 1988–7 July 1989), Fairchild's 92d BMW (from 15 June 1988), Altus' 340th AREFW (from 16 June 1988), March's 22d AREFW (from 1 July 1988), Castle's 93d BMW and Dyess' 96th BMW (both from 15 July 1988) and Francis E. Warren's 90th SMW (from 23 August 1988).

SAC headquarters directly controlled Offutt's 544th SIW (throughout), McConnell's 384th AREFW (from 1 July 1987) and Wurtsmith's 379th BMW (from 8 June 1988).

SAC Directorate of Space and Missile Warning Systems

Until 1979 Aerospace Defense Command (ADC), a USAF MAJCOM, had been responsible for providing strategic air defence forces within the contiguous USA, including space surveillance and missile warning systems. On 29 March 1979 the USAF announced ADC would be inactivated and its assets distributed to three other USAF MAJCOMs. Management of active interceptor units, ground-based air defence radars and control centres would be transferred to Tactical Air Command (TAC); communications resources to Air Force Communications Command (AFCC); space surveillance and missile warning resources would pass to SAC. SAC absorbed these elements by 1 December 1979, forming SAC's Directorate of Space and Missile Warning Systems. SAC only retained these assets until 1983, when they were transferred to newly activated MAJCOM, Space Command.

The four AN/FPS-50 early warning radar antennas, making up part of the Ballistic Missile Early Warning System, of the 12th MWG at Thule Site J. (NARA)

BMEWS technicians of
the 12th MWG in the
Tactical Operations Room
at Thule. (NARA)

The Ballistic Missile Early Warning System (BMEWS), operational since 1960, provided ICBM early warning. BMEWS radars were located at three sites – two under SAC control. These were operated by 12th Missile Warning Group at Thule Site J, near Thule AB, Greenland, and 13th Missile Warning Squadron, at Clear Air Force Station (AFS), Alaska. The third site was operated by the RAF at RAF Fylingdales, UK, and directly linked into the network.

Another ICBM warning system was the AN/FPQ-16 PARCS (Perimeter Acquisition Radar and Characterization System). Originally developed as the Perimeter Acquisition Radar (PAR) under the US Army's Safeguard anti-ballistic missile (ABM) system, this site (with Sprint and Spartan ABMs) became operational on 1 October 1975; however, Congress terminated the project the next day. The USAF subsequently took over PAR, as PARCS, using it for early warning of incoming ICBMs at ranges up to 2,000 miles (3,200 km). PARCS was operated by 10th Missile Warning Squadron at a facility called Concrete Missile Early Warning System (after the nearby town of Concrete, near Grand Forks, North Dakota), renamed Cavalier AFS in 1983.

BMEWS (and later PARCS) faced north, looking for Soviet ICBMs on direct trajectories over the northern Polar Regions. However, the 1960s Soviet development of the Fractional Orbital Bombardment System (FOBS) bypassed such warning mechanisms. While regular ICBMs travelled on a direct ballistic trajectory from launch to target, a FOBS missile entered a fractional orbit, travelling further and approaching the target from any direction, including via the southern hemisphere (the opposite direction to existing ICBMs). The Soviet R-36orb (SS-9 Mod 3 Scarp) FOBS missile entered service in 1968–69. To counter this threat the AN/FPS-85 Spacetrack Radar was developed and installed at Eglin AFB Site C-6, Florida. Operational since 1969, it was operated by 20th Missile Warning Squadron. The world's first large (and most powerful) phased array radar, it faced south with 120° azimuth coverage.

While Spacetrack largely negated the threat of FOBS, a further threat arose with improved SLBM-equipped Soviet SSBNs entering service in increasing numbers in the 1970s. To counter this threat, PAVE PAWS (Precision Acquisition Vehicle Entry, Phased Array Warning System) was developed utilising AN/FPS-115 phased array radars (two radars in a large three-sided structure per site). Two sites were initially established.

Above: An aerial view of the 6th MWS PAVE PAWS radar site at Cape Cod AFS in 1980. (NARA)

Left: A staff sergeant monitors a radar scope at the 6th MWS PAVE PAWS radar site in 1982. (NARA)

The 6th Missile Warning Squadron, activated at Cape Cod AFS, Massachusetts, on 1 October 1979, reaching IOC on 4 April 1981. The 7th Missile Warning Squadron at Beale AFB, California, also activated in 1979, reaching IOC on 15 August 1981. Two further sites were developed after SAC passed responsibility on to Space Command.

SAC also became responsible for sites dedicated to tracking Soviet ICBM tests. The 16th Surveillance Squadron at Shemya AFB operated the AN/FPS-108 'Cobra Dane'

Security policemen patrol the area around the 16th SS's AN/FPS-108 'Cobra Dane' radar system at Shemya AFB. (NARA)

long-range early warning radar system, used for tracking and gathering intelligence on Soviet ICBM test launches.

The 19th Surveillance Squadron at Pirinçlik Air Station, Turkey, used the AN/FPS-17 Space Surveillance Radar to detect objects in space with fixed antennae oriented towards the Soviet rocket launch and development site at Kapustin Yar, and the FPS-79 UHF tracking radar, capable of tracking Soviet missile tests.

On 1 September 1982 Space Command activated, absorbing SAC's space surveillance and missile warning operations (by 1 May 1983), plus AFSC's space launch operations.

Air Training Command (ATC) and Military Airlift Command (MAC) support

ATC supported SAC's Accelerated Co-Pilot Enrichment (ACE) Program (providing bomber/tanker co-pilots additional flying hours to maintain skills) via T-37 trainer detachments at SAC bomber/tanker bases.

MAC's 37th Aerospace Rescue and Recovery Squadron (ARRS) provided helicopter detachments to (primarily ICBM) SAC bases. The following 37th ARRS Dets operated HH-1Hs throughout the 1980s, unless stated otherwise: Det 1, Davis-Monthan (inactivated on 30 July 1984); Det 2, Ellsworth (UH/TH-1F until 1986, HH-1Hs thereafter); Det 3, Grand Forks; Det 4, Little Rock (inactivated on 18 August 1987); Det 5, Malmstrom (UH/TH-1F until 1987, HH-1Hs thereafter); Det 6, McConnell (inactivated on 31 July 1986); Det 7, Minot; Det 8, Vandenberg (with UH-1Ns); Det 9, Whiteman (UH/TH-1F until 1984, HH-1Hs thereafter); Det 10, Francis E. Warren (UH/TH-1F until 1987, HH-1Hs thereafter); Det 24, Fairchild (active 1 November 1987–1 June 1989, supporting the USAF Survival School. This previously operated 1 July 1978–1 November 1987 as Det 24, 40th ARRS).

End of an Era

President Bush directed SAC to take all bombers, tankers and ICBMs off continuous alert on 27 September 1991, following the Cold War's de facto conclusion, and several months after SAC had been heavily committed to the Gulf War. The USAF was soon completely reorganised. SAC inactivated on 1 June 1992. SAC's former bomber, reconnaissance and ABNCP aircraft and ICBMs joined former TAC assets in newly activated Air Combat Command (ACC); most SAC tankers were transferred to the new Air Mobility Command (AMC). ICBMs soon transferred again, to Air Force Space Command (AFSPC). By 1995 there were five Bomb Wings and five (ICBM) Missile Wings/Groups. B-1Bs adopted an exclusively conventional tasking; B-52Hs, joined by B-2As, had a dual nuclear/conventional tasking. Peacekeepers were withdrawn by 2005, leaving Minuteman IIIs the sole ICBMs.

On 7 August 2009 a new MAJCOM, Air Force Global Strike Command (AFGSC), activated, holding SAC's lineage, history and honours. Initially absorbing ACC's B-2As/B-52Hs and AFSPC's Minuteman IIIs, B-1Bs joined AFGSC in 2015; E-4Bs following in 2016. At the time of writing AFGSC includes five Bomb Wings (two B-1B, one B-2A and two B-52H) and three Minuteman III Missile Wings.

Bibliography

Archer, Bob, *Super Snoopers* (Fonthill Media Limited, 2020)

Bell, Dana, *USAF Colors and Markings in the 1990s* (London: Lionel Leventhal Limited, 1992)

Berhow, Mark A., *US Strategic and Defensive Missile Systems 1950–2004* (Oxford: Osprey Publishing, 2005)

Cole, Ronald H., *Operation Just Cause* (Washington: Joint History Office, Office of the Chairman of the Joint Chiefs of Staff, 1995)

Cole, Ronald H., *Operation Urgent Fury* (Washington: Joint History Office, Office of the Chairman of the Joint Chiefs of Staff, 1997)

Crickmore, Paul F., *Lockheed Blackbird, Beyond the Secret Missions (Revised Edition)* (Oxford: Osprey Publishing, 2016)

Donald, David, and Lake, John (eds.), *Encyclopedia of World Military Aircraft Volumes 1 & 2* (London: Aerospace Publishing Limited, 1994)

Donald, David (ed.), *US Air Force Air Power Directory* (London: Aerospace Publishing Limited, 1992)

Dorr, Robert F., and Peacock, Lindsay, *B-52 Stratofortress: Boeing's Cold War Warrior* (Osprey Publishing 1995)

Francillon, René J., *The United States Air National Guard* (London: Aerospace Publishing Limited, 1993)

Graham, Richard H., *SR-71 Revealed* (Minneapolis: Zenith Press, 1996)

Hopkins III, Robert S., *Strategic Air Command in the UK* (Manchester: Hikoki Publications Limited, 2019)

Hopkins III, Robert S., *The Boeing KC-135 Stratotanker: More Than a Tanker* (Manchester: Crécy Publishing Limited, 2018)

Pocock, Chris, *50 Years of the U-2* (Atglen: Schiffer Publishing Ltd, 2005)

Rogers, Brian, *United States Air Force Unit Designations since 1978* (Hinckley: Midland Publishing, 2005)

Schlosser, Eric, *Command and Control* (London: Penguin Books Ltd, 2013)

Walmer, Max, *Strategic Weapons* (London: Salamander Books Ltd, 1988)

Yenne, Bill, *The Complete History of US Cruise Missiles* (Forest Lake: Specialty Press, 2018)

Journals and Periodicals

World Air Power Journal, various volumes (Aerospace Publishing Limited)

Unpublished Papers

Callaway, Lane, 'SAC Bomb Comp – History Chronology and Factoids' (8 AF/HO, 2009)

Hopkins, J. C., and Goldberg, Sheldon A. , 'The Development of Strategic Air Command 1946–1986' (Offutt AFB, Nebraska: Office of the Historian, Headquarters Strategic Air Command, 1986)

Myers, MSgt Gary P., 'The Story of the 544th Strategic Intelligence Wing 1950–1985' (November 1985)

'Peace... is our Profession: Alert Operations and the Strategic Air Command, 1957–1991' (Offutt AFB, Nebraska: Office of the Historian, Headquarters Strategic Air Command, 1991)

'Seventy Years of Strategic Air Refueling 1918–1988: A Chronology' (Offutt AFB, Nebraska: Office of the Historian, Headquarters Strategic Air Command, 1990)

Appendix I

SAC Structure January 1980

HQ Offutt AFB, NE

Direct Reporting

10th MWS (Concrete Missile Early Warning System, ND)
(Operating AN/FPQ-16 PARCS, providing early warning of incoming ICBMs)

20th MWS (Eglin AFB Site C-6, FL)
(Operating AN/FPS-85 Spacetrack Radar)

544th SIW (Offutt AFB, NE)

1st Strategic Aerospace Division (Vandenberg AFB, CA)

4315th CCTS (Vandenberg AFB, CA)
(ICBM training unit – assigned directly to 1st Strategic Aerospace Division)

3d Air Division (Andersen AFB, Guam)

43d SW (Andersen AFB, Guam)
60th BMS – B-52D
(43d SW also controlled TDY KC-135s)

376th SW (Kadena AB, Okinawa, Japan)
909th AREFS – KC-135A/Q
(Plus TDY RC-135M/V)

7th Air Division (Ramstein AB, West Germany)

19th SS (Pirinçlik AS, Turkey)
(Operating AN/FPS-17 and FPS-79 radar to track Soviet missile tests)

11th SG (RAF Fairford, UK)
Controlled TDY KC-135As deployed to Fairford
Det – TDY KC-135As (Keflavik, Iceland)

306th SW (RAF Mildenhall, UK)
Controlled TDY KC-135A/Q and RC-135s deployed to Mildenhall
34th SS – TDY KC-135As (Zaragoza AB, Spain)
922d SS – TDY KC/RC-135s (Hellenikon AB, Greece)

Eighth Air Force, Barksdale AFB, LA

19th Air Division (Carswell AFB, TX)

2d BMW (Barksdale AFB, LA)
62d BMS – B-52G
596th BMS – B-52G
71st AREFS – KC-135A
913th AREFS – KC-135A

7th BMW (Carswell AFB, TX)
9th BMS – B-52D
20th BMS – B-52D
4018th CCTS – B-52D
7th AREFS – KC-135A

340th AREFG (Altus AFB, OK)
11th AREFS – KC-135A

381st SMW (McConnell AFB, KS)
532d SMS – LGM-25C
533d SMS – LGM-25C

384th AREFW (McConnell AFB, KS)
91st AREFS – KC-135A
384th AREFS – KC-135A

40th Air Division (Wurtsmith AFB, MI)

12th MWG (Thule AB, Greenland)
(Operating BMEWS)

305th AREFW (Grissom AFB, IN)
70th AREFS – KC-135A, EC-135G/L
305th AREFS – KC-135A

351st SMW (Whiteman AFB, MO)
508th SMS – LGM-30F
509th SMS – LGM-30F
510th SMS – LGM-30F (Including ERCS-equipped missiles)

379th BMW (Wurtsmith AFB, MI)
524th BMS – B-52G
920th AREFS – KC-135A

410th BMW (K. I. Sawyer AFB, MI)
644th BMS – B-52H
46th AREFS – KC-135A

42d Air Division (Blytheville AFB, AR)

19th BMW (Robins AFB, GA)
28th BMS – B-52G
912th AREFS – KC-135A

68th BMW (Seymour Johnson AFB, NC)
51st BMS – B-52G
911th AREFS – KC-135A

97th BMW (Blytheville AFB, AR)
97th AREFS – KC-135A
340th BMS – B-52G

308th SMW (Little Rock AFB, AR)
373d SMS – LGM-25C
374th SMS – LGM-25C

45th Air Division (Pease AFB, NH)

42d BMW (Loring AFB, ME)
69th BMS – B-52G
42d AREFS – KC-135A
407th AREFS – KC-135A

380th BMW (Plattsburgh AFB, NY)
528th BMS – FB-111A
529th BMS – FB-111A
4007th CCTS – FB-111A
310th AREFS – KC-135A/Q
380th AREFS – KC-135A/Q

416th BMW (Griffiss AFB, NY)
668th BMS – B-52G
41st AREFS – KC-135A

509th BMW (Pease AFB, NH)
393d BMS – FB-111A
715th BMS – FB-111A
509th AREFS – KC-135A

Fifteenth Air Force, March AFB, CA

4th Air Division (Francis E. Warren AFB, WY)

28th BMW (Ellsworth AFB, SD)
37th BMS – B-52H
28th AREFS – KC-135A
4th ACCS – EC-135A/C/G

44th SMW (Ellsworth AFB, SD)
66th SMS – LGM-30F
67th SMS – LGM-30F
68th SMS – LGM-30F

55th SRW (Offutt AFB, NE)
1st ACCS – E-4A/B
2d ACCS – EC-135C

38th SRS – RC-135M/U/V, RC-135T
343d SRS (No aircraft – provided mission back-end crews for 38th SRS RC-135 ops)
[Wing also operated C-135A CSA, KC-135A CINCSAC VIP transport and KC-135A
(ARR) trainer]

90th SMW (Francis E. Warren AFB, WY)
319th SMS – LGM-30G
320th SMS – LGM-30G
321st SMS – LGM-30G
400th SMS – LGM-30G

12th Air Division (Dyess AFB, TX)

22d BMW (March AFB, CA)
2d BMS – B-52D
22d AREFS – KC-135A

96th BMW (Dyess AFB, TX)
337th BMS – B-52D
917th AREFS – KC-135A

390th SMW (Davis–Monthan AFB, AZ)
570th SMS – LGM-25C
571st SMS – LGM-25C

14th Air Division (Beale AFB, CA)

9th SRW (Beale AFB, CA)
1st SRS – SR-71A/B, T-38A
99th SRS – U-2R, U-2CT, T-38A
Det 1 – SR-71A (Kadena AB, Okinawa, Japan)
Det 2 – U-2R (Osan AB, South Korea)
Det 4 – U-2R, SR-71A (RAF Mildenhall, UK)
Det 5 – SR-71A (Eielson AFB, AK)
OL-OH – U-2R (RAF Akrotiri, Cyprus)

93d BMW (Castle AFB, CA)
328th BMS – B-52G/H (aircrew training unit, secondary operational mission)
93d AREFS – KC-135A (aircrew training unit, secondary operational mission)
924th AREFS – KC-135A
4017th CCTS (KC-135/B-52G academic training)

100th AREFW (Beale AFB, CA)
9th AREFS – KC-135Q
349th AREFS – KC-135Q

320th BMW (Mather AFB, CA)
441st BMS – B-52G
904th AREFS – KC-135A

47th Air Division (Fairchild AFB, WA)

13th MWS (Clear AFS, AK)
(Operating BMEWS)

16th SS (Shemya AFS, Aleutian Islands)
(Operating Cobra Dane long-range early warning radar system)

6th SW (Eielson AFB, AK)
24th SRS – RC-135S, RC-135T (Plus TDY KC-135s)

92d BMW (Fairchild AFB, WA)
325th BMS – B-52G
43d AREFS – KC-135A
92d AREFS – KC-135A

341st SMW (Malmstrom AFB, MT)
10th SMS – LGM-30F
12th SMS – LGM-30F
490th SMS – LGM-30F
564th SMS – LGM-30G

57th Air Division (Minot AFB, ND)

5th BMW (Minot AFB, ND)
23d BMS – B-52H
906th AREFS – KC-135A

91st SMW (Minot AFB, ND)
740th SMS – LGM-30G
741st SMS – LGM-30G
742d SMS – LGM-30G

319th BMW (Grand Forks AFB, ND)
46th BMS – B-52H
905th AREFS – KC-135A

321st SMW (Grand Forks AFB, ND)
446th SMS – LGM-30G
447th SMS – LGM-30G
448th SMS – LGM-30G

Appendix II

SAC Structure January 1989

HQ Offutt AFB, NE

Direct Reporting

379th BMW (Wurtsmith AFB, MI)
524th BMS – B-52G
920th AREFS – KC-135A

384th BMW (McConnell AFB, KS)
28th BMS – B-1B
384th AREFS – KC-135R

544th SIW (Offutt AFB, NE)

Eighth Air Force, Barksdale AFB, LA

2d BMW (Barksdale AFB, LA)
62d BMS – B-52G
596th BMS – B-52G
2d AREFS – KC-10A (Activated 3 January 1989)
32d AREFS – KC-10A
71st AREFS – KC-135A

7th BMW (Carswell AFB, TX)
9th BMS – B-52H
20th BMS – B-52H
7th AREFS – KC-135A

19th AREFW (Robins AFB, GA)
99th AREFS – KC-135R
912th AREFS – KC-135R, EC-135N/Y

68th AREFW (Seymour Johnson AFB, NC)
344th AREFS – KC-10A
911th AREFS – KC-10A

97th BMW (Eaker AFB, AR)
340th BMS – B-52G
97th AREFS – KC-135A

305th AREFW (Grissom AFB, IN)
70th AREFS – KC-135A/D/R, EC-135G/L
305th AREFS – KC-135A/D/R

351st SMW (Whiteman AFB, MO)
508th SMS – LGM-30F
509th SMS – LGM-30F
510th SMS – LGM-30F (Including ERCS-equipped missiles)

410th BMW (K. I. Sawyer AFB, MI)
644th BMS – B-52H
46th AREFS – KC-135A
307th AREFS – KC-135A

416th BMW (Griffiss AFB, NY)
668th BMS – B-52G
41st AREFS – KC-135A

7th Air Division (Ramstein AB, West Germany)

11th SG (RAF Fairford, UK)
Controlled TDY KC-135As deployed to Fairford
Det – TDY KC-135As (Keflavik, Iceland)
34th SS – TDY KC-10As (Zaragoza AB, Spain)

17th RW (RAF Alconbury, UK)
95th RS – TR-1A/B

306th SW (RAF Mildenhall, UK)
2d SS – TDY tankers and RC-135s deployed to Mildenhall
922d SS – TDY KC/RC-135s (Hellenikon AB, Greece)

42d Air Division (Grand Forks AFB, ND)

319th BMW (Grand Forks AFB, ND)
46th BMS – B-1B
905th AREFS – KC-135A/R

321st SMW (Grand Forks AFB, ND)
446th SMS – LGM-30G
447th SMS – LGM-30G
448th SMS – LGM-30G

45th Air Division (Pease AFB, NH)

42d BMW (Loring AFB, ME)
69th BMS – B-52G
42d AREFS – KC-135A/R
407th AREFS – KC-135A/R

380th BMW (Plattsburgh AFB, NY)
310th AREFS – KC-135A/Q
380th AREFS – KC-135A/Q

528th BMS – FB-111A
529th BMS – FB-111A
530th CCTS – FB-111A

509th BMW (Pease AFB, NH)
393d BMS – FB-111A
715th BMS – FB-111A
509th AREFS – KC-135A

Fifteenth Air Force, March AFB, CA

22d AREFW (March AFB, CA)
6th AREFS – KC-10A (Activated 3 January 1989)
9th AREFS – KC-10A
22d AREFS – KC-135A

90th SMW (Francis E. Warren AFB, WY)
319th SMS – LGM-30G
320th SMS – LGM-30G
321st SMS – LGM-30G
400th SMS – LGM-118A

92d BMW (Fairchild AFB, WA)
325th BMS – B-52H
43d AREFS – KC-135A
92d AREFS – KC-135A

93d BMW (Castle AFB, CA)
328th BMS – B-52G (aircrew training unit, secondary operational mission)
93d AREFS – KC-135A/R (aircrew training unit, secondary operational mission)
924th AREFS – KC-135A
329th CCTS (KC-135/B-52G academic training)
330th CFIS (Taught B-52 and KC-135 Combat Flight Instructors Courses)

96th BMW (Dyess AFB, TX)
337th BMS – B-1B
338th CCTS – B-1B
917th AREFS – KC-135A

301st AREFW (Malmstrom AFB, MT
91st AREFS – KC-135R

340th AREFW (Altus AFB, OK)
11th AREFS – KC-135R
306th AREFS – KC-135R

341st SMW (Malmstrom AFB, MT)
10th SMS – LGM-30F
12th SMS – LGM-30F
490th SMS – LGM-30F
564th SMS – LGM-30G

1st Strategic Aerospace Division (Vandenberg AFB, CA)

4315th CCTS (Vandenberg AFB, CA)
(ICBM training unit – assigned directly to 1st Strategic Aerospace Division)

4392d ASW (Vandenberg AFB, CA)
(Operated the base at Vandenberg)

3d Air Division (Hickam AFB, HI)

43d BMW (Andersen AFB, Guam)
60th BMS – B-52G
65th SS – TDY KC-135s and B-52s

376th SW (Kadena AB, Okinawa, Japan)
909th AREFS – KC-135A/Q
(Plus TDY RC-135V/W)

12th Air Division (Ellsworth AFB, SD)

28th BMW (Ellsworth AFB, SD)
37th BMS – B-1B
77th BMS – B-1B
28th AREFS – KC-135R
4th ACCS – EC-135A/C/G

44th SMW (Ellsworth AFB, SD)
66th SMS – LGM-30F
67th SMS – LGM-30F
68th SMS – LGM-30F

14th Air Division (Beale AFB, CA)

6th SRW (Eielson AFB, AK)
24th SRS – RC-135S, TC-135S (plus RC-135X from July 1989)
(Plus TDY KC-135s)

9th SRW (Beale AFB, Ca)
1st SRS – SR-71A/B, T-38A
5th SRTS – U-2R(T), TR-1B, T-38A
99th SRS – U-2R, TR-1A, T-38A
349th AREFS – KC-135Q
350th AREFS – KC-135Q
Det 1 – SR-71A (Kadena AB, Okinawa, Japan)
Det 2 – U-2R (Osan AB, South Korea)
Det 3 – U-2R (RAF Akrotiri, Cyprus)
Det 4 – SR-71A (RAF Mildenhall, UK)
Det 5 – U-2R (Patrick AFB, FL)

55th SRW (Offutt AFB, NE)
1st ACCS – E-4B
2d ACCS – EC-135C
38th SRS – RC-135U/V/W, TC-135W

343d SRS (No aircraft – provided mission back-end crews for 38th SRS RC-135 ops)
55th MCCS (Survivable/road-mobile/truck-based backup command post)
[Wing also operated C-135A/NKC-135A CSA, KC-135E CINCSAC VIP transport and KC-135E (ARR) trainer/support aircraft]

320th BMW (Mather AFB, CA)
441st BMS – B-52G

57th Air Division (Minot AFB, ND)

5th BMW (Minot AFB, ND)
23d BMS – B-52H
906th AREFS – KC-135A

91st SMW (Minot AFB, ND)
740th SMS – LGM-30G
741st SMS – LGM-30G
742d SMS – LGM-30G